T0123587

Blow Your Nose

to work smarter | live freely
| create legacy

Susanne Moore, RN, JD

ARCHWAY
PUBLISHING

Disclaimers: The author is not a mental health professional and opinions expressed herein are simply that, opinions. If the reader is in distress, please seek professional help immediately. All names used in the following pages are fictional and the stories may have been modified to protect identities.

Archway Publishing books may be ordered through booksellers or by contacting:

Archway Publishing
1663 Liberty Drive
Bloomington, IN 47403
www.archwaypublishing.com
844-669-3957

Because of the dynamic nature of the Internet, any web addresses or links contained in this book may have changed since publication and may no longer be valid. The views expressed in this work are solely those of the author and do not necessarily reflect the views of the publisher, and the publisher hereby disclaims any responsibility for them.

Any people depicted in stock imagery provided by Getty Images are models, and such images are being used for illustrative purposes only. Certain stock imagery © Getty Images.

ISBN: 978-1-6657-4845-2 (sc)
ISBN: 978-1-6657-4846-9 (e)

Library of Congress Control Number: 2023915202

Print information available on the last page.

Archway Publishing rev. date: 09/07/2023

DEDICATION

Thank you to my daughters Alex and Milena who always remind me to have fun and stop doing things "the hard way." Thank you to past connections with others who taught me to get out of my head and into my heart. To them I owe that I am continuing to work on intuition and intentional productivity, as opposed to incessant busy-ness. To them I owe appreciation for learning interdependence over extreme independence. Because of all of you, I am now able to accomplish so much more, yet in a kinder and infinitely better way.

PREFACE

Do you want your life to continue to be nothing more than an accomplishment driven adrenaline see-saw? Are you exhausted from chasing success? Do you want to feel deeply, connect strongly, have fun, feel care-free, while still accomplishing more than you ever thought possible?

Remember when you were little, and you had a runny nose? Your mom chased you around with a tissue saying, "stop and blow your nose" and all you really wanted to do was keep playing and sniffing, completely annoying everyone else?

As an adult, I run in the cold. One chilly morning I was running trails in the woods with a couple of friends. We were all sniffing. Something about running when it's cold opens all the passageways in an uncontrollable and messy manner. We had been talking about emotions and difficult relationships and the struggle of working past them. In that moment we had a group epiphany.

Human nature, even as adults, tempts us to sniff back our runny noses. None of us wanted to stop running long enough to find a tissue in our packs to blow our noses. Instead, we kept running and sniffing and running and sniffing. Breathing heavily while fighting with the same blurb of mucous for miles. (And equally annoying each other with the sounds.)

Running at a fast clip is infinitely harder when you need to blow your nose. Getting enough oxygen is a real challenge. You are having to breathe much harder to run the same distance and speed. In short, it is counterproductive.

The unchanneled "busy-ness" found by so many of us Type A, ultra driven, highly motivated or adrenaline junkie individuals is the same way. We push, we fight, we grind and usually we do it the hardest way.

We ignore our emotions, our fatigue, our fear, and we just go. And go and go and go. It works. Until it doesn't. At some point, it typically runs straight into the arms of burn-out, substance abuse, broken relationships, damaged health, feelings of isolation or sometimes loss of the ability to feel at all.

Running through life as fast and as hard as we can with bottled up sadness, loneliness, fear, anger, or resentment is essentially like trying to breathe through a mucus blob. It's hard. It holds us back. And it's annoying to the people in our life.

Breathe freely. Live freely. Create legacy.

free·ly
['frēlē]
ADVERB

1. not under the control of another; as one wishes:
   "I roamed freely"

   o without restriction or interference:
      "air can freely circulate"
   o in copious or generous amounts:
      "she drank freely to keep up her courage"

synonyms:
copiously · plentifully · amply · profusely · exuberantly · prolifically ·

○ openly and honestly:
"you may speak freely"
synonyms:
openly · candidly · frankly · plainly · matter-of-factly ·

○ willingly and readily; without compulsion:
"I freely confess to this failing"
synonyms:
voluntarily · willingly · readily · of one's own volition ·

leg·a·cy
[ˈleɡəsē]
NOUN

1. the long-lasting impact of particular events, actions, etc. that took place in the past, or of a person's life:

Living intentionally in a way that causes your life to continue to contribute to others long after you pass.

CONTENTS

Chapter 1 Coming Alive 1

Chapter 2 Releasing Limiting Beliefs.................................6

Chapter 3 Find Your Power through Emotional Triggers............18

Chapter 4 Questions Are Hugs for the Brain 32

Chapter 5 Apocalyptic Feelings 46

Chapter 6 Forging a Way Out of Limbo 56

Chapter 7 Spin It Till You Win It 63

Chapter 8 Well, Hello, Shadow Side...................................71

Chapter 9 Secrets Kill (and So Do Narcissists) 78

Chapter 10 Brain Inflammation, Impulsivity and Addiction....... 83

Chapter 11 Good Vibrations and Mindset............................ 92

Chapter 12 The Mirror (Facing Short Term Pain Erases
Long Term Suffering)....................................... 101

Chapter 13 Using Empathy to Be a Really Good Human 107

Chapter 14 Yes, Teens are Lovable and Trustable (Are You?).....116

Chapter 15 Attachment Theory 124

Chapter 16 The Five Factors for Feeling Full 135

Chapter 17 The Hardest Things are also the Easiest.................... 142

Chapter 18 Abundant Thinking 163

Chapter 19 Lessons from Kevin and Kyle 167

Chapter 20 Who Do You Want to Be................................. 173

CHAPTER 1

Coming Alive

As a child, I remember my father frequently having rages of anger and yelling at us. Sometimes these rages would go on for hours. I had no defense, no real way to cope with or fix the situation. My natural survival response therefore was to tune it out. Had I truly listened to his words, my child mind would not have been able to cope with the trauma. Therefore, I would mentally turn him off, like I was turning off a light switch or a faucet. I disassociated completely from the situation. His mouth was still moving but I was no longer present. In this state I would watch his facial contortions with interest. It became rather amusing to me. I knew he would never physically strike me. He simply did not know how to handle his own triggers and fears, so he verbally raged. The ability to "turn off" the uncomfortable stimuli as a child was extremely helpful from the standpoint of survival. Whereas my other family members were emotionally scarred from his outbursts and toxicity, I felt rather fine. I let them roll right off me. I was proud of my thick skin, my resilience, my imperviousness to his hostility.

These childhood survival traits later served me well in the workplace. I was able to handle criticism constructively. I was not bothered by workplace drama. I was able to handle enormous pressure and deadlines with ease. I was exceedingly proud of my ability to perform like a machine, like a surgeon, no matter what storm was raging around me. My accomplishments made me feel good and powerful and in control, so I kept chasing one after another.

The downside to this extreme self-control and independence did not manifest until years later...in relationships. The reality is that we are the sum of ALL our emotions. ALL our feelings. When we shut down and disassociate from the difficult or uncomfortable ones, we similarly shut down and disassociate from the positive ones, without even realizing it.

I mostly felt adrenaline, or the lack thereof, the thrill of project completion or the lack there of, and a constant need to be busy. I needed a continual stream of goals, projects, tasks, and objectives. On this I thrived. Ask me to sit calmly in the living room with family, friends and small talk for an afternoon and I wanted to crawl out of my skin. Ask me to play cute games with my children and it was a struggle for me. My mind was racing on other things. Ask me to go on a date with my husband and, unless there was an objective like planning a trip or learning a new skill, I struggled. I could not simply "be."

I was a highly responsible and nurturing parent, but not a very emotionally involved one. I was the master at planning my children's lives and making sure they had the best food, sleep, exercise, education, and opportunities but rarely did I simply sit with them and listen. What did they think and like and want and dream? I was oblivious to this. I was focused on crafting them into what I thought they should be. Productive, competent, responsible humans.

A series of traumatic life events helped me see the light. As is often the case for most of us, it took pain to force me to slow down and emotionally mature. A series of deaths of loved ones very close to me brought me to a place I had never been. For more than one of those deaths, I felt guilt. I felt that had I paid more attention and asked more questions I may have been able to prevent the death. This haunted me. I played back conversations where one of these individuals had opened up to me and, like most avoidants, I was dismissive. I deflected because it felt unnatural to me to go deep into someone's emotions with them. I wanted to tell them they were ok or tell them what I thought they should do or tell them what I would do in their shoes. Instead, what I should have said was, "I'm very sorry you are going through this. What can I do to best support you? What is your plan? I am here for you." So simple. So easy. A mere choice of words can have the massive effect of reassuring someone rather than making them feel less than. How could I have not known?

On another of the deaths, the individual needed medical treatment but refused to go. I told them the grim medical consequences of their decision. I was forceful. I pleaded. I pushed. I pulled. I offered to make the appointment and take them. They refused. They died. Perhaps all I needed to do was hold their hands, look in their eyes and say "I understand that you are not going to go. I do not understand why but I am certain you have your reasons. I would like to better understand those. Are you comfortable sharing them with me? I am here to support you whatever you decide."

Some of the most accomplished individuals I know struggle the most with connecting and with simply "being." We task addicts and productivity junkies thrive on our to-do lists and check marks, while sometimes bulldozing those around us. Although it feels good to "do" so much, do you ever feel anxious that maybe you aren't doing the most important things you should be? The ones that are harder to check off the list? The ones that involve listening, connecting, sharing, creating?

Living freely is about letting go of the addiction to being in control, ultra busy and always right. It's about being able to listen, be curious, have fun and let magic in.

Creating legacy is about looking past today's to-do list and considering who do you want to inspire and who do you want to be remembered as. What do you want to be remembered for? Whose life do you want to change and in what way? It's ok to stay on the hamster wheel. But just for a minute, pause on it and let's explore possibilities.

Have you ever looked at someone you viewed as far less accomplished than you and for just a moment felt a blink of jealousy? Because you saw that their responsibilities did not rule their life? You saw that their need to manage everything did not crush their ability to have fun. You saw that they could be carefree, while you felt the need to always be productive and on top of things?

Being productive, independent, and accomplished are great things. Things to be proud of. But if those traits have slowly grown to drain the soul from you, then this book is for you. You can keep your powerful traits, while releasing all the compartmentalized feelings you trapped along the way and regaining your intuition, so that you can allow yourself to feel, to play, to discover and to be spontaneous.

Creating legacy requires that we create more than we consume. To be creators requires that we connect with ourselves, our higher source, and others. This is because to be creative requires that we receive. It requires that we be willing to receive inspiration, ideas, and purpose, rather than live in the silo of our own brain. To connect and to receive requires that we release our ego and increase our capacity for empathy.

If you feel like you are trapped on the productivity /task hamster wheel, without necessarily creating real value, you are in the right place. If you feel anxious that you are not actually doing what you were meant to do in life, this book is for you. If you would like to become more creative and better at connecting with and lifting others up, this book is for you. If you want to find meaning and leave a real legacy, this book is for you.

Through the quizzes and questions in this book you will get to know your personality on a whole new level. You will start seeing conflicts with others as fun opportunities instead of triggers. You'll start to productively use your emotions to benefit you (rather than compartmentalizing them). You'll stop letting the hamster wheel be your task master and you'll level up to be more of a creator and less of a consumer.

CHAPTER 2

Releasing Limiting Beliefs

OUR BEHAVIORS WILL ALWAYS BE PREDICTED BY OUR BELIEFS about ourselves. This is simply the truth. There is no way around it. To change our lives, we must change our behaviors. To change our behaviors, we must first change our underlying beliefs.

Our beliefs are formed from what we are told as children and what we tell ourselves. They are formed by the information we consume and the circles in which we run. For many of us, we were taught that we had to work hard to succeed. That we had to make opportunities happen. That everything worthwhile was a struggle. Some of this is true, but it is only part of the story.

Years ago, as a young lawyer I was working on extra projects on the weekends to pay off school debts. I was working 7 days a week, had been doing so for years and felt like my progress was incredibly slow. In search of a better path, I began attending a John Maxwell Masterminds group that a friend had started. As we worked our way through the 21 Irrefutable Laws of Leadership, I began feeling the block in my mind begin to lift. I began practicing the principles and possibilities began to unfold. One day I received a random recruiting call from a national company, offering me a high level leadership opportunity at three times my current salary. I was stunned. This had never happened in my life. I called my friend, stunned, and excited. She calmly said, "Yes, you opened your mind to the universe bringing you possibilities and it delivered. That's how it works." I went on to stammer about how I did not think I was qualified for this position and how did they find me and why would they have called me. At the same time, it sounded like my dream job. She calmly listened again and then said only three words, "Why *not* you?" Indeed. Why not me. Three words I had never considered. I took a deep breath and for the next several days repeated to myself, "Why *not* me."

I interviewed for the job and was offered the amazing salary contingent on flying to the company and meeting all the leadership. A couple weeks later the position fell through due to an unexpected company restructuring. Yet, the experience was life changing. I learned my true salary market value and saw myself and my potential in a completely different way. For the first time in my life, I realized that with the right mindset, good things could flow TO me, rather than me always chasing them. A few weeks later I was cold- called by another company. When they asked my salary requirements, I knew exactly what to say. I told them the same number the first company had offered me. They hired me. Had the first call not happened I would have significantly undersold myself. Even more astonishing, it was the only two times I have ever been cold call recruited, and both happened shortly after making the commitment to open my mind and possibilities to better career opportunities through a mastermind class. I didn't polish up my resume and apply to a hundred jobs. I didn't go to a headhunter company. I changed my mindset and let the universe know I was ready to grow into a bigger role.

I do not profess to understand the law of attraction or synchronicity, yet I do know this, it works. When you open your mind and soften your demeanor, becoming faithful to the premise that if you show up and commit, the universe will rally the resources to support your mission, something magical does happen. I have experienced it time and time again. Sometimes the way we make the most progress is by stopping the hustle for a moment and listening, looking, and following the signs we are given.

Why would we ever let our own limiting beliefs, such as thinking we have to work hard for every good thing, hold us back from all that's possible?

Case study. My friend is an MD who married a small-town business owner. She had traveled the world; he had been born and raised in the same small town. They adored each other. As her prominence in the medical community rose, she was offered increasingly higher-level positions. Finally, one was a Medical Director position in another state. It was what she had always dreamed of. They moved into a beautiful new home, had upper-class friends, began to travel and life seemed great. Until it didn't. You see, his belief about himself was that he was an uneducated small-town farm boy. Even though he was extremely intelligent and personable and capable, because he believed he was "just" a farm boy, he could only see himself in that lifestyle. He was still running his business remotely and now had free time, a steady income, great credit and connections. The sky was the limit. But his brain, because of his belief systems, said otherwise. His brain said, "You don't belong here." "You are not supposed to be in a big house, with free time and opportunity and travel. You're supposed to be in a small house, living a simple life, working hard to make a living. None of this feels right." He wasn't consciously aware of this. All he knew was that he felt anxious and unhappy and depressed. He began blaming it on his wife. It was her fault she took away the life he was accustomed to living. It was her fault she was busier now with her more important job. It was her fault his days were less busy. He believed he couldn't really do anything, because after all, he believed he was only capable of one type of career and one type of lifestyle. He didn't believe he deserved this exciting new life. So, he sank lower and lower into his state of victim. His behavior soon began to mirror the toxic beliefs. He began drinking and hiding truths and secretly acting out. She sensed the change in personality and, feeling uncertain, withdrew more into work. He sank lower. Ultimately, no amount of encouragement could change the situation because he neither recognized nor wanted to change his beliefs. The behaviors continued, finally culminating in divorce and him moving back to the small town.

None of this had to happen.

What needed to happen was for the underlying limiting beliefs to be replaced by new beliefs. If he had seen his own ability as others saw it, if he had believed in himself, his behavior would have been much different. This level of insight is not something we are automatically good at on our own. This is why so many successful people in the world have psychologists and coaches. It is not easy to sort through the spirals of our own thoughts and find clarity.

Identifying our beliefs, so that we can change them, is key to creating the life we want.

Recently I saw an episode of *Selling Sunset*. In the episode, the glamorous real estate agent is describing her new marriage to a wealthy tech mogul and moving into her dream home. She says something to the effect of "I manifested this. I sat in that home showing it as a real estate agent and I pictured myself drinking coffee there, in that kitchen, my kitchen." It sounds hokey, but it's true. She believed she was worthy. So she dressed and acted the part long before she had a wealthy husband and the home. We attract who we see ourselves as and who we believe we are.

If we want to be around a different class of people, we first have to see ourselves as them, then dress and live like them.

There is a saying: "Dress for the job you want, not the job you have." It's true, partially because of the appearance you create but even more because of the mindset you adopt, which then automatically shifts your behaviors and attracts different people and circumstances to you.

This theory applies also to our loved ones. If you want your child to start being more responsible, start treating them as though they already are. Notice the tiniest things they do that are responsible and excitedly praise those. Tell them how responsible they are (even if they aren't yet). This will grow and grow.

Telling people what to do, or what not to do, really never works. Humans like to do what they want. Watch for the behavior you want to see more of, and say, "Wow, I love how you (*Example, took out the trash*) You are becoming such a (*responsible*) person."

This is the Baader-Meinhof phenomenon. Have you ever noticed that if you're thinking about buying a white Mercedes, you start seeing them everywhere? If you start thinking your partner is cheating on you, you may start seeing "clues" everywhere, even if they're not cheating.

If you focus on someone's faults, you'll see more of them. You might start to nag them, chipping away at your relationship. If you believe in the best that you see, you'll notice their great qualities more. As you praise those, the person will do those more. Your relationship will deepen. It all starts with what belief you choose to adopt and nurture.

I recently saw a dad who had been very close to his daughter when she was young but was seemingly distant from her as a teen. I was surprised by the change in dynamic and began asking questions. He shrugged his shoulders and said, "She doesn't need me anymore." What a sad resignation. What really happened is that this dad did not evolve with his daughter. As she grew into a teen, her need for him did not go away, it simply changed. Because he was not willing to see that, and to grow into the dad he would need to be to support her as a teen, he simply walked away. He chose a preemptive strike. He created a belief in his own mind that she no longer needed him and decided he was doing her a favor by going away quietly. That was the path of least resistance for Dad, but it certainly was not what he or his daughter needed. What she needed was for him to lean in. To get to know the evolving person she was becoming and to evolve with her. To listen to her and to seek knowledge on how to better meet her ever-changing needs. His self-created limiting belief caused him to miss an opportunity to become even closer to her and to help her know she could count on the men in her life to always be there for her. Instead, she was left thinking men are there when things are convenient and easy (like when she was a cute 8-year-old) and will disappear when things become more challenging or messy.

How do you know what your limiting beliefs are, so that you can work on them?

Start by writing a list of what you believe.

> *What do you believe about your finances?*
> *Your career?*
> *Your education?*
> *Your marriage?*

On a scale of 1 to 10, how do you feel about each of those areas right now? Why? What would it take to make each one a 10? What could you do today, right now, to start?

Write it all down. Is it what you want? If not, write what you do want.

Make it specific. Make it realistic yet bigger than what you think you can have. Visualize it. Imagine you have it now. How is your daily life different? What aspects of that daily life can you incorporate now? Watch how your behaviors change as your beliefs change.

Here's an example. Let's say you literally can't stand your boss or teacher. They drive you crazy. Maybe you believe they are total jerks out to get you.

Write down a changed belief where you identify a new truth. Perhaps it's one thing you do like about them or one possibility that could explain their poor behavior.

I believe my boss Joe has anger issues that may have come from a tough childhood. He drives me crazy. However, I love how he always keeps his desk super neat and makes the team follow rules.

Now focus only on that. Make sure it's truthful. Every time your brain wants to take the lazy path of thinking about what a jerk Joe is, gently think, yes that may be true but ... and replace the thought with your new belief. Watch the magical difference this makes in lowering your stress at work and improving your productivity and relationships. It's so simple but so incredible how quickly it can change how you react to the other person and, over time, how they treat you.

Years ago, I remember reading one of Tim Ferris's first books. I was fired up and motivated by some of his concepts. I was walking and talking with one of my good friends, who also happens to be a business coach. I was raving about some of the concepts in the book and I said,

"I'd love to meet Tim Ferris and just pick his brain for an hour." She looked at me with utter seriousness and said, "Who would you have to become that he would want to meet you first?" I stopped dead in my tracks. That line of wisdom has followed me ever since, changing the way I think and who I am becoming. Why do we limit ourselves by assuming others are better than us? If we think that is true, why do we not identify how we think they are superior and then work on becoming our own version of our best? It is a compelling challenge. To not accept the status quo version of who you are today, but rather envision who you could evolve into tomorrow, next year, next ten years. Notice she did not say, "What would you have to DO?" She said, "Who would you have to become?" Yes.

Think about who you want to meet, where you want to live, what you want your life to look like. Write it down. Who do you have to become that those visions would become your reality? Kinder? Stronger? Braver? More authentic? Now define how you could start that journey today.

For me, I had to stop the hamster race of doing and start learning to "be." I had to learn to stop searching externally for achievements and challenges and start searching internally for my most authentic self. There I would ultimately find my creativity, my ideas, my ability to truly love and my capacity for true joy and fulfillment. Today, I find that while I am still fired up by the adrenaline from productivity and achievement, I am also thrilled with the simple acts of playing games with my kids, drinking a delicious latte or asking a teenager what is important to them. I have learned to both "do" and to "be." With that has come a sense of contentment and, surprisingly, ideas for even bigger goals. A sense that my goals are no longer to prove something to my ego or to others, but a feeling that my goals are to fill a need, to solve a problem, and to build value in the world. I no longer feel the anxiety of the rat race. Instead I feel that every day is a gift and I'm excited every day to see what words I can speak and what actions I can take to give that gift to others. I am curious about other's stories.

This change in belief related to who we are and why we do what we do brings gratitude. Without a doubt, the state of gratitude attracts more abundance. We are often told to keep a gratitude journal. Although this can be a useful exercise, the state of gratitude needs to become far deeper than a check list. It should be the very frequency from which we radiate. A state of mind that is continuously in wonder at all the things around us.

To release a limiting state of mind and place myself into gratitude, I use touch. I'll use my finger to gently trace and feel something, slowly, softly. For example, the computer mouse. I'll take a moment to really see it, to recognize that in this tiny device is the power to bring my words to life on the computer screen, words which can then come to life in books read by millions. The act of gently tracing the outline of the computer mouse is a surprisingly powerful way to go into a gratitude state over the smallest thing. Suddenly I appreciate technology, our modern world, my fingers, my mind. I feel a sense of magic, like anything is possible. Sometimes on my way to work, I'll use my finger to trace the steering wheel. I find I am quickly transferred to a state of wonder that I am driving, that we have cars, that I am healthy enough to drive, that I am going to a job I love, that I live in a first world country with women's rights. Each idea races to the next. It is truly a mind state where great peace and relaxation settles and creative energy flows. It is a state of expansion and love, pushing away contraction and fear.

To take this deeper, I have found the following exercise to be incredibly freeing.

I put myself in child's pose (a yoga position) and verbalize an issue I am struggling with and then I state the following: "Thank you universe, for helping me see what I need to see, hear what I need to hear, understand what I need to understand and do what I need to do." I say the words slowly, purposefully. When I finish, I find myself more alert and observant. I am tuned in. The information flows to me, without any need of mine to search for it or force it. I simply know what I need to do.

I once gave this advice to a friend who was struggling in her marriage. Her heart and stomach told her something was "off" and she was no longer in a safe environment. Her mind kept rationalizing what a good, kind, and loyal person her husband was, and it must be her who needed to "get her head on straight." She was unable to be intimate with him and did not know why. She felt guilty, stressed, anxious and scared. Every time she was with him, he acted normally, and she had to assume something was wrong with herself. She didn't know what to do but the limbo state she was in was destroying them both.

This went on for weeks. One day, while he was outside, she followed my advice and did the above exercise. When she finished, she stood up and saw something for the first time. His Apple watch, laying on the bedside table. A voice inside said, go look at it. Her rational mind laughed. "Don't be ridiculous, he is the most loyal person ever. Plus, you have looked at his phone before and there has never been anything concerning on it." She had never owned an Apple watch and had never used one. She slowly picked it up, not even knowing what buttons to hit or what to do. The voice gently encouraged her. Look, search. She began pushing buttons. Soon she found dozens of text messages from multiple women. It was all right there. Months of lies and deceit. Her heart and gut were right.

When she confronted him, he was shocked. He said he thought he had deleted everything. He had…from his iPhone. The universe always comes through, if we believe that it will and we relax into a state of humble gratitude, thanking it for things yet to happen.

In this exercise, notice I do not ask the universe for any specific outcome. This is the key. Rarely do we know what outcome is best for us. We are selling ourselves short if we ask for what we think we want.

How many times have you desperately wanted a certain relationship or situation to work out, only to realize years later that it was an great blessing that it did not? Trust in the process, not the outcome. Thank the process for guiding you right where you need to be, to grow the most.

LIMITED THINKING

I agree there is a great deal of true diagnosable trauma and mental health conditions. But I also think we have a lot of cases of "limited beliefs and contracted thinking" that cause symptoms we sometimes mistake as a mental health condition.

Mankind has ALWAYS struggled to be motivated, to be positive and to do the hard things.

In centuries past, this was not as apparent, due to sheer necessity. If you wanted to eat, you had to work, and work very hard to survive. Rarely was there some mechanism to bail you out. You had to go to work whether you "felt" like it or not and if you wanted anything more than a bare existence, you had to work for it.

At the same time, work was finite. When the sun went down, you had to stop working outside.

Now, because basic survival has become easier, some people struggle with motivation. At the same time, because of electricity and the internet, for others, it has become harder to turn tasks "off."

There is a balance there and finding your optimum place lies in clearly defining what you want your life to look like, defining what limiting beliefs are holding you back from that, and developing a path forward.

Although most of us want to think that sheer willpower is the key to changing our life, it's not. First, we must go deep to see what lives in our internal emotional basket. There is where we will find the place where our decisions and behaviors come from.

What is one thing you are struggling with right now? Is it your weight? Your partner? Your job? Your finances?

Write it down. What do you think is causing that struggle? Ask yourself what that is? To that answer, ask yourself why again? Get very clear on this one issue and the deep internal root underlying it. Our goal by the end of this book is to solve it. We are going to call it the Thing. Because the more you release your Things, the more energy you have to create and give.

CHAPTER 3

Find Your Power through Emotional Triggers

HAVE YOU EVER FELT THAT RUSH OF INTENSITY THAT FLOODS over you when something "triggers" you? Like when you're already late for work and you see traffic is backed up ahead? Or when your teen is late coming home again and your worry is out of control? Or your partner says, "We need to talk." What if, instead of emotional triggers causing us discomfort, they became the basis of our identity and power? The underlying source of almost all conflict and pain comes from expecting others to notice our emotions, understand our emotions, and resolve our emotional state for us. How frustrating is it to be in a relationship, to be a parent or child, to be an employee or boss and struggle with the other person not treating us the way we wish to be treated? What if there was a way to end these desperate feelings quickly and easily? What if there was a way to make calm, rational decisions and set solid action steps to gain the life and the relationships we want, with clarity and focus? There is.

There is a way to quickly find clarity, comfort, and power, in every situation, through your own emotional triggers.

Why does it matter?

Emotions are guideposts to living an authentic life. Learning how to use them fully is the key to learning who you are and connecting deeply to your talents. Becoming the most authentic version of you means fulfillment, confidence, impact. It means tapping into your creativity, your passion. It means finally finding and developing the personality traits that make you who you are.

Emotions are to your brain what nerves are to your physical body. Nerves are what cause you to feel pain when you touch a hot stove. Emotions alert your brain that you are in a situation that could threaten or violate your core traits or beliefs.

Sometimes we need to overcome our nerves. For example, while running a marathon. In that instance, you may want to override pain to accomplish your goal. Emotions are the same. Once you truly feel and honor their warning system, you can decide how you want to handle them. Instead of reacting (which is letting your emotions run your life), you can follow an intentional process to use your emotions as guideposts to align you to the core traits and beliefs most important to you. You become in control of them, and you use them as the tools they are meant to be.

Triggers

What ARE triggers? Have you ever felt a wave of emotion flood you? Anger or resentment or sadness or fear? The wave of emotion is your guidepost being activated, your life authenticity alarm bell. The trigger is the scenario that activated the alarm bell.

Triggers are waves of emotion that flood over us when one or more of the core traits, beliefs or associations most important to us is being activated. Negative waves of emotions mean we feel our core need is being threatened or violated. Positive waves of emotions mean one or more of our core traits are being met. Much in the way nerves alert us to pain to keep us from danger, negative emotions alert us that we are in situations that do not align with our core beliefs and traits. Positive emotions alert us that we ARE in situations that align with core beliefs and traits, but even these situations need analysis. More on this in the case studies below.

An event that triggers one person may have no effect on another. This is because each person has their own specific core beliefs and traits. This is part of what makes us unique individuals. Our feelings about an event are very individual to us, depending on what unique traits make up who we are. Have you ever tried, in a conflict, to make someone understand exactly how you feel? This is why it's so hard.

Once you are in touch with the guideposts of your emotions, you can use them positively. Rather than expecting the other person or a change in the situation to resolve your painful feelings, you'll be able to self-soothe your feelings yourself.

Directing your internal emotional reaction toward another person is usually pointless. It is YOUR emotion. It is unique to you. How you react to events is unique to the filter from which you view the world. This filter has evolved from your genetics, your childhood, your environment, and events that have happened in your life. Another person will not intuitively understand your raw emotional reaction because they do not share your identical traits and core beliefs. As a result, their filter and their perception are different.

How you feel is completely your own personal responsibility. All the other person needs to know is your calmly stated feeling and your boundary. All you need to know from them is whether they are willing to respect this once you express it. If not, and if it is significant enough, you may need to move on and detach from this person or situation. Practicing this gives you your power. On the other hand, uncontrolled emotional outbursts (or bottling our emotions) strip us of our power and leave us feeling desperate and confused.

The first step is identifying your core traits. Here are a few examples. Circle the three that most resonate with you:

Acceptance	Respect	Be Liked	Be Understood	Be Needed
Be Valued	Attention	Comfort	Freedom	Peacefulness
Balance	Consistency	Order	Variety	Love
Safety	Predictability	Be Included	Fun	New Challenges
Autonomy	Control	Be Right	Be Treated Fairly	Purpose

Really spend some time thinking about this and pencil in your three choices:

_____   _____   _____

Our core traits are what make us so special and unique because they are not only what make up who we are, they are the gifts we give back.

If your core traits are to be in *control* and *be right* and have *order,* you may make a great leader and that is your gift that you bring to the world. You can let it have full rein at work, but you may need to relax that need to be part of a team in relationships. If your core need is to feel *needed* and *valued* and *included,* that is how you will make others feel and how incredible is THAT gift?

This is why it is so important to become aware of what our core traits are so we can honor them and give these gifts to others. At the same time, think of them as an elastic band. They are not rigid. They can stretch and give. For example, maybe a core need for *attention* and to give *attention* is fantastic in a job as a day-care worker, but you may need to temper it when you are in other settings. Truly gaining power over core traits means we embrace them and protect them, without becoming a slave to them. They begin to serve you and others, rather than you mindlessly reacting to their pull.

Core Beliefs. What core beliefs affect you? Here are just a few examples. Feel free to write in your own.

- I must do everything myself, no one else will take care of me.

- If I am disciplined about my diet, my cleanliness, my habits, my friends, I will be successful.

- I can't trust people.

- I need to work hard. Nothing comes easy.

- I am unlovable, no one will ever appreciate, take care of me.

- I am unworthy, others will reject me. I will fail. I am useless.

- If I assert myself or my true traits, people will not like me. They may abandon me.

- _____(write in your own)

Core Associations

Sometimes we have associations underlying our core beliefs. As an example, a person may have an association that certain genres of music are low class. This is an association tied to a core belief that to be successful, a person must listen to certain music or dress a certain way or have certain habits or friends. We all have a multitude of associations, some of which serve us and some of which no longer serve us. Once we recognize the ones that no longer serve us, we can gently release them so we can live more balanced lives.

The reality is most of us do not recognize the core limiting beliefs and associations we have. These beliefs and associations in turn create thoughts and feelings. Because some of these thoughts and feelings are uncomfortable, most of us have spent years running from our emotions, numbing our emotions, or dumping our emotions onto others expecting them to make us feel better.

Why do we do this? Because underlying most of our uncomfortable feelings is some form of fear. Fear feels awful. We don't like it. So, we try to escape it. At its root, anger comes from fear. And depression is anger turned inward. Fear itself comes from the feeling that our physical needs or our emotional core traits are being threatened. These uncomfortable feelings of anger, fear and depression are scary and it is easy to want to remove them by substance abuse, being addicted to work, shopping, sex, food, consuming excessive distracting entertainment or being overly dramatic. What if, though, these feelings are incredibly important and what we really need to do is to deeply understand them?

In the following method, our goal is to slow down, feel the wave of emotion and fully sit in that emotion long enough to do the work the emotion is asking us to do. It's being self-aware of our core traits, beliefs and associations and understanding how it is THOSE things that are causing the wave of emotion, much more so than the situation. It is understanding that because of this, we can develop a way to process our feelings quickly and fully honor our needs, without relying on events or other people for our happiness, comfort, and fulfillment.

Practice: Before you use this method, it is important to become adept at feeling your feelings. Few of us naturally know how to do this. To start on a piece of paper, write down a lie and write down a truth on paper. For example, "I hate ice cream. I love my grandmother." Then say the first one out loud. Say it a couple of times if needed and visualize. What do you feel? Expansion or contraction? Relaxation or tension? In your shoulders? Stomach? Face? Knots? Butterflies?

Now say the truth. What does that feel like? Do you feel your shoulders or face relax? Think of it and say it out loud. What do you feel?

The STEADY Method

When you feel the triggering wave of emotion, rather than reflexively reacting to the triggering person or event, the first step of the method is to quietly sit in the emotion and fully feel it. What is this feeling? Where is it truly rooted? Fully feel it. What does it feel like in your body?

The second step is to thank the emotion for alerting you to the situation. Tell yourself that you will take care of the situation. Remind yourself that you trust yourself enough to take care of you. Tell yourself you trust yourself to place boundaries to protect your core traits. Once you have reassured yourself that you will address the situation, allow the emotion to gently process through. Its work is done. Then calmly review these questions to determine your course of action.

1)   Is it a core trait, belief, or association worth keeping? Does it serve you in this setting?
2)   Is the threat significant enough to warrant taking action?

Let's break it down with a case scenario:

1) Triggering event: *Example, family member leaves dirty clothes on the floor again.*
2) Triggered emotion: *Wave of anger and frustration.*
3) Identify the core trait or belief that feels violated or threatened. *A need for control, order, respect?*
4) Internal Response:
   a) Out loud, thank the emotion for alerting you to a triggering of your core need.
   b) Decide whether the core trait or belief is one you wish to keep.
   c) Decide whether the situation is truly a threat to your core trait or belief, one worth fighting for. Decide whether it warrants setting a boundary. Will setting this boundary meet your need?
   d) Honor your feelings and reassure yourself that you will address the situation. Trust yourself to meet your traits. Focus on what you feel and why, ignoring for the moment what the other person did and your assumptions regarding why. Allow the emotion to gently process through. Once you feel calm and centered, then move to the External Response.
5) **External Response Person A:** *Hey, when I see your clothes on the floor, I feel disrespected and anxious. I have a high need for order and cleanliness, to the extent that I am not able to feel relaxed and loving when my environment is messy. I want to feel respected and relaxed and loving. This may seem silly, but it is a very important need to me. What are your thoughts?*
6) **External Response Person B:**
   a) "I had no idea this created these feelings in you. Absolutely, I'll start picking them up and if I forget please gently remind me."
   b) "You are not the boss of me. I can do whatever I want. You should get over your feelings." If "b" is the response, Person A now has a choice to make. She can either consider leaving this person who clearly does not respect her feelings and traits,

or decide the trigger is not worth losing her relationship over and release her attachment to her need for order regarding the bedroom setting. She could also hire a maid. She is in control. She has the power. She decides but no matter her decision, she honors her need. She also understands that the reason her family member does this is not because he is personally trying to attack or disrespect her. It is because his core traits are different, and cleanliness does not rank high on his. This is simply a difference.

It's about compassion and curiosity, both toward self and others. It eliminates blame, judgment, criticism, passive-aggressiveness, and manipulation. It eliminates the feelings of desperation and panic. It is a way to honor and meet one's traits, and understand the traits of another, from a place of compassion and curiosity. It is a way to know when to remove yourself from an unacceptable situation.

The acronym STEADY helps us work through each step.

STEADY METHOD

Sit in the emotion.

Thank yourself for this alert, this emotion. Feel gratitude.

Express reassurance to yourself. Honor your core traits. Relax and trust yourself.

Accept and analyze which core trait is being activated. Which belief. Which association?

Decide your action.

You can decide to release attachment to the core trait for this moment or calmly set a boundary.

Your core traits matter. They are your gifts and part of what makes up your personality.

Sometimes it is important to sit in the feeling long enough to determine whether it comes from a past event or a current one. The other person will always interpret your reaction as coming from a current event. Reacting badly toward them because of memories will only confuse them if they are not aware of what is triggering your reaction. In addition, the past cannot be changed, so it is more important to release those old feelings, so they do not color your current situations.

Your feelings are ALWAYS valid. Your thoughts, conclusions and reactions to your feelings often are not. For example, feeling sad is valid. Thinking "I am worthless" because I feel sad is not valid and having this thought means we need to sit in the sad feeling and spend some time better understanding and honoring it, so the thought can be replaced with a more valid one, such as "I am sad and sometimes that is normal and I just need to process it." Thank the feeling and trace it back to its true origin, so you can do the work to gently release it, using the method. Once you are skilled in the method, your reactions will come from a calm, centered, rational place. You will still achieve what you need, but in a way that works.

Here are some real-life examples.

FEAR OF PUBLIC SPEAKING

People who have a fear of public speaking have a predictable response. They feel intense anxiety, manifesting as tightness in the chest or throat, knots in the stomach, dry mouth or difficulty breathing. These are all symptoms of the fight or flight system activating. This system is primal within us and was a survival mechanism so that we could escape life or death situations. So why does the mere act of speaking in front of other people trigger this intense nervous system response? And how do we alleviate it?

The first step is identifying which of your three core traits is feeling threatened by the thought of public speaking. Is it fear of rejection because being valued is important to you? Is it fear of criticism because being appreciated is important to you? Is it fear of someone disagreeing with you because having peace is important to you? Is it simply that you haven't spent time preparing yet? Spend some time thinking through what you are feeling and what core trait is being triggered.

Once you have identified the physical feeling in your body and the core trait that is threatened, work through the steps of the STEADY Method.

In this case, keep in mind that the intense feelings in your body are occurring because your mind does not know the difference between a real life or death threat and the perceived threat of criticism or rejection.

Ask yourself this. If the life of the person you most loved hinged on whether you could stand in front of a crowd and give an impassioned speech, could you do it then? Would your need to save your loved one's life overpower your own ego-driven fear? Of course, it would! Now ask yourself this, if the topic of your speech was something so powerful that you know it would positively impact and change people's lives, perhaps save people's lives, then could this motivation overcome your own ego-driven fear? Yes!

Recognize that the feelings in your body are intense because your mind thinks this is a life-or-death threat. But it's not. That simply isn't true. Even if your need to be valued is strong, can you cope with the fact that some of the people in the audience may not like what you say or how you speak? Of course, you can. Is it life or death for you? No.

Picture speaking in front of a crowd and try to fully feel all the intense feelings that flood over you. Gently acknowledge, honor, and release them, recognizing that this is not a life-or-death situation. Find the value in what you are going to say and allow that mission to override your reaction.

What is something you have always wanted to do, that you thought you couldn't? Can you apply this process to that?

FEEL GOOD TRIGGERS

Not all triggers evoke uncomfortable emotions. Some evoke exhilarating emotions. Ironically, those can be even more dangerous and need our awareness and analysis before reacting.

A classic case is Amy, a typical teenage girl in love with a tattooed up bad boy. Although hormones are at play, what makes Amy choose him over the straight-A quarterback all-star who also works a job after school? Our core values always drive our behaviors. If a core value for her is to feel loved, and she is not receiving that sufficiently at home, she may be overwhelmed with positive emotional triggers when he says all the right words. If another core value is autonomy and she is feeling micromanaged at home, it may also be a way for her to feel she has control of her own life. These are incredibly strong drives, almost as strong as your drive to pull your hand from a hot stove or eat a warm chocolate chip cookie even though you're already full of dinner.

This explains why no matter how much you try to use logic with her, it will flow in one ear and out the other. The inner drive to fulfill her core need is going to drive her decision and behavior over all logic. Our emotional survival wiring is that strong.

The only way a parent can effectively approach this is to connect with Amy's core values, rather than pick a fight with her intellect.

Our instinct as parents comes from a place of fear. We instantly think of how sad her life may become if she stays with this guy. We think of all the worst outcomes. He may not provide for her. He may use her. He may have children with her and not take care of them. He may treat her badly or cheat on her. We are overwhelmed with our own fear and panic at the possibilities.

This causes in us an immediate reaction to lecture her, control her, stop her from going down this path.

And yet, it is the worst possible reaction. Essentially, without being aware of it, by being with him, Amy is seeking to fulfill her own core needs. You telling her she is wrong, is basically you telling her that her identity is flawed. She will, out of pure emotional survival, push back with the weight of all the world's mountains. It would be like trying to force her to stop eating for two weeks. You can't do it. She will lie, cheat, steal, run away and fight to get food. As she should. Her survival depends on it.

So, what can you do?

Go deep into the why with her.

Hey, Amy, I see you are becoming close to Joey. What does he make you feel like? Let her answer. How does he do that? Let her answer. Do you see yourself with him five years from now? What do your friends think of you being together? What is your biggest concern about being with him long term? What do you feel are the core values that most resonate with you? Do you feel like we, as your family, help you meet those? How could we meet those needs in a better way? What is your vision of your perfect future life? Do you feel like Joey will enable you to have that? How will he do it?

These questions can't happen as an interrogation. They must happen organically, in bite-size chunks. She has the answers. Your job is to help her ask herself the right questions.

Once we learn to honor these emotions so we can protect and selflessly give of our traits, we are able to live more freely and focus more on pouring into others and creating legacy.

CHAPTER 4

Questions Are Hugs
for the Brain

ONE OF THE GREATEST WAYS TO CREATE LEGACY IS TO FIND THE most effective ways to support others. The memories they will have of how you inspired or encouraged them will be there forever.

Have you ever wondered what the best way is to help friends and family deal with anxiety, depression, or anger? Sometimes, the answer is in seeking professional mental health care. But that's only part of the solution. This is because there is a big difference between mood control / emotion regulation and true diagnosable mental health conditions. Some of the sadness, anxiousness and anger we see is simply the ongoing struggle all of us have at times in managing our feelings and triggers. It takes effort and habit formation to learn how to effectively manage moods. Life is sometimes difficult. For everyone. Life is naturally full of stressors and challenges and loss and grief.

Learning how to cope with life events in a graceful and calm manner occurs through the development of emotional maturity. Yet developing emotional maturity is not an easy process. It is often a very painful process.

Learning how to help others cope with intense emotions, and grow in emotional maturity, is best achieved by empathy. Two significant ways to express empathy are hugs, which are physically supportive, and questions, which are mentally supportive.

Seeing a loved one, especially a child or spouse, experiencing intensely uncomfortable emotions can be draining and difficult. It is hard to know what to do. It's normal to feel a strong need to "fix" their issues for them, but that only takes away their power and perpetuates the cycle. There is also often a strong desire to talk them "out of their feelings." Nothing is more impossible. Feelings are feelings. They are not necessarily rational, and, in the heat of the moment, they cannot be resolved by intellect or rationalization, nor should they be.

The truth is, the most helpful thing we can do is to validate that they feel what they feel, and then empower them to find their own solutions.

We do this by showing them we support them and by asking the right questions. Then we listen. We restrain the need to tell them what we think they should do. We override the urge to tell them how we handled our last bout of sadness! We stop thinking and talking. And we simply listen. In that moment, THEIR perspective is the one that matters. It does not matter if it is right or wrong or whether it makes sense to us or does not.

When someone we love is depressed, and we are reactive, they may retreat deeper. When we show genuine support, without enabling or "fixing," we empower them to want to find their own solutions. Over time, as they practice their solutions, they become stronger. This is how to help someone develop emotional maturity. Through support, listening and gentle redirection.

Here are examples:

Person A: "I am so depressed. I feel worthless. I'm such a burden to everyone. I never do anything right."

Supporter: Provide a hug, if appropriate. Then you can say: "I hear you. I am here. I have seen you work through these feelings before. What do you think is triggering these feelings?" Let them vent. Say little. Followed by: "What would help you feel better? What has helped you before?" Often, they know exactly what they need to do. Encouraging them to say it out loud helps them. If they say something that someone else needs to do, redirect them to what they can do themselves, in the here and now. Example: If they say, "It would help me feel better if my boyfriend would be more considerate," your response could be, "Yes, I am sure that would help. But it is possible he may not change. If that's the case, what can you do for yourself to feel better right now?" It also helps to remind them that feelings are like storms. They pass. And that you are going to stick with them until this one passes, too.

We can all be a part of the solution, every day. The next time you are with someone who is experiencing anxiety, sadness, anger, you can commit to being the person who empowers them to find their way.

Questions to Ask Someone Who is Suffering

Humans are pack animals. Pack animals look out for each other. We all have a responsibility to let others be heard. Rather than try to fix someone's issues, depression, anxiety, grief, or anger, ask questions to stimulate them to find their own solutions and forge their own path.

How are you feeling today?

What action could you take that would make today better?

How can I best support you?

When was the last time you felt great? What triggered that? How could you recreate that? Who would you have to become to create that?

What do you need from me?

What does it feel like?

What thoughts are haunting you? What works best for you to deal with thoughts like this?

If I could change one thing for you right now, what would it be?

Where does your strength come from?

What makes you feel empowered?

How have you gotten through this before?

Questions are hugs for the brain anytime though, not just when someone is experiencing difficult emotions. Keep a list of questions in your mind to build others up anytime.

Questions to Ask Your Inner Self

"The MOST important thing is to become self-aware." Gary Vaynerchuk.

This exercise is designed to dig into what is in your heart and who you want to become. On each of these questions keep asking "why" to each of your answers until you are as deep as you can possibly go.

Who am I destined to be?

What should I read to guide my path?

Who should I talk to in order to guide my path?

What would my daily life look like, if I were living up to the truest, most authentic version of myself and my capabilities?

To continue this journey, "Never go to sleep without a request to your subconscious." Thomas A. Edison. Every night before drifting to sleep, ask yourself a question you would like answered or a problem you would like solved. This can be as simple as "Where did I leave the remote?" to "How can I become debt free?" Continue asking the same question or posing the same problem nightly until it is solved.

Most of us spend a substantial amount of time wrapped up in our own thoughts, trapped in our heads, recycling an endless stream of thoughts related to what we do not like and what we do not want. None of this is productive. Let go of pointless rumination and focus on controlling and steering your thoughts and feelings.

Who do I have to become to be of my greatest value possible to society?

How can I start today?

Questions to Ask Your Boss

If you could change anything about my work performance, what would it be?

What is the one thing I could do differently during my workday that would really improve my value to you?

Questions to Ask Yourself

What would be my ideal career?

Why?

Who would I have to become to do that?

Who should I interact with and what education can I undertake to start that journey?

What were my childhood goals and dreams?

Can I pick one now, and do it? If not, why not?

Who are the five people I spend the most time with?

Does each person build me up?

Does each person challenge me?

Does each person inspire me?

Do I build each of my five people up?

What action could I take today to challenge, inspire, or build up one of my five people?

Who do I look up to?

Why?

What action step could I take today to become more like them?

Do I believe in a higher power?

If yes, do I harness that power in my life?

How?

How could I harness it more?

What is the one food I could add to my diet to make me feel better?

What is one area I am struggling in? What if I approached it completely differently for forty-eight hours? Tim Ferriss tells a remarkable story about this. After months of struggling in his first job out of college, which was selling data storage to CEOs and CTOs, he decided to experiment with doing the opposite of all the other sales reps. He made his sales calls from 7:00 a.m. to 8:30 a.m. and 6:00 p.m. to 7:30 p.m., rather than between 9:00 a.m. and 5:00 p.m. He asked questions instead of pitching. And he studied technical material to sound like an engineer rather than a sales guy. "The experiments paid off," he writes. "My last quarter in that job, I outsold the entire LA office of our biggest competitor."

I wish _____fill in the blanks_____

Why?

What is stopping you?

What could you do today to start?

Fortune favors the bold. In the words of Tim Ferris: "The best results I have had in my life, the most enjoyable times, have all come from asking the simple question: What is the worst that could happen?"

Who do you want to become?

Why?

Why is that important?

What could you do today to start that path? What would you have to sacrifice to do so?

Why would it be worth it?

One way to look at this is to think about it in terms other than just "goals." What would excite you every day? What kind of life would make you want to leap out of bed at 4 a.m. every day because you simply could not wait to get started? For most people, it would not be a life of luxury. It would be a life of great meaning, significance, and purpose. Going through this journey of mindfulness and questions will help you find that path.

What is the ONE thing you could do this year that would have a big impact for you?

Why?

Why is that important to you?

Do those I love know unequivocally that I love them?

How?

What step could I take today to show that more completely?

What step could I take today to save money?

What step could I take today to start becoming debt-free?

What book idea do I have right now?

What invention idea do I have right now?

What is keeping me from acting on it?

What is one product I can think of that could be improved?

What would the improvement be?

What is one simple problem that could be easily solved with an invention?

Why should anyone be led by me?

What if ... I were told that I was destined for greatness? How would I begin preparing? How would each day look different than it does now?

The next three questions are from Tony Robbins and can be found at the below link. www.tonyrobbins.com/masterpiece/ask-better-questions/

1. What is something I can do for someone else today?
2. What is something I can do to add value to the world today?
3. What is something that I have to offer other people?

"If you routinely ask these questions, you will begin to frame the way you experience the day completely differently. Rather than your mental and emotional state being the product of external forces, you will see how you can begin to shape the world around you. Rather than asking what you are getting from something or someone, you will start to ask yourself what value you can bring to the table. You will begin to approach different events and circumstances in a way that encourages problem-solving, contribution and growth. You will begin to see the gifts that you have to offer others and the positive impact you are able to make on the world around you." www.tonyrobbins.com/masterpiece/ask-better-questions/ 9.4.2017

Generally Great Questions

Tim Ferris has spent much of his career finding out what makes top performers tick. He has found that their biggest commonality is ... of all things ... asking absurd questions. Absurd questions have a unique power. They trigger breakthroughs. They break out of constraints to encourage limitless thinking.

For a great example, when entrepreneurs ask author, entrepreneur, and brilliant businessman Peter Diamandis for his investment advice, he responds with a question: "How can you increase the economics of your business by a factor of 10 in the next three months?" If they say "impossible," he does not accept that.

Here are some generally great questions.

What was your last dream?

How did it make you feel?

If you could go forward in time, what time period would you go to?

To see what, and why?

If you could have any career what would it be?

Why?

What is your earliest childhood memory?

How does it make you feel?

Do you believe in mermaids?

Based on what?

Do you believe in aliens?

Based on what?

What is your favorite place you have ever visited?

Why?

These questions are the tip of the iceberg. According to billionaire innovator Elon Musk, "Really we should aspire to increase the scope and scale of human consciousness in order to better understand what questions to ask." *Elon Musk: Tesla, Space X, and the Quest for Fantastic Future* by Ashlee Vance.

Questions to Ask Kids

The Would You Rather game is an excellent tool for developing children's self-awareness and creativity. The key to this game is to go deep. For each answer they provide, ask why. Keep asking why until you are at least six or seven levels deep. Game changer.

Would you rather?

Have money or wisdom? Why? (Keep asking why to each answer.)

Be an astronaut or a doctor?

Read or watch TV?

Have one very close friend or five somewhat close friends?

Fail at a big undertaking or never undertake anything that could cause you to fail?

Have a hug or a handshake?

Invest money or save money?

The **What If** game is also extremely stimulating and provokes possibilities and limitless thinking.

What if?

What if I told you that you were destined to be a great teacher (*insert any career here)*, the greatest teacher there has ever been? How would it make you feel? Would you want to begin preparing now? What would you do differently today? How would you start? Would you like to start learning about great teachers? How could you do that? Where would you start?

What if I told you that you could learn a foreign language in ninety days? Would you want to start? Would you be willing to commit thirty minutes a day for ninety days?

What if I told you that you could learn to build your own app in ninety days? Would you want to start? Would you be willing to commit thirty minutes a day for ninety days?

And another good set of questions:

> Who did you help today?
> Who helped you today?
> What caused a pang?
> What felt good?
> What did you fail at today?

The first time I asked a bunch of middle schoolers these questions in the car one day, they were hesitant at first. After a few days, they began reminding me to ask them! We all love to be asked questions.

Asking questions is a hug for the brain, deepens connections, and takes us one step closer on our journey from ego to empathy.

Questions to Ask Your Significant Other

Do you feel loved unconditionally by me? How?

Do you feel supported? What would make you feel (more) supported? What is one thing you did today to be better than you were yesterday?

What is the ONE thing we could do every day that would take less than ten minutes but would make us stronger? It could be emotionally, spiritually, physically, or mentally. Every thirty days, change this one thing.

Ideas for this one thing: one minute of plank followed by one minute of sit-ups, joint prayer, joint guided meditation, massage, foot massage, reading an inspiring book, idea drafting.

What motivates you most?
If you had the power to affect change in any area of society you wanted, what would it be? What could you do today to start?

What makes you cry? Why does that make you cry? Keep asking why to every answer until you are as deep as you need to go.

What is the one thing you wish I would do? Why?

What do you need from me?

What is one thing you could achieve that would make you feel great about yourself?

Have you ever gone into a relationship expecting the other person to "make you feel better," "take care of you" or "help you feel whole?" A relationship is not meant for any of those purposes. It is meant to be a tool for growth. With a partner, you should feel a little more secure and safe to take risks and develop yourself more. It is each person's full duty to manage their own feelings, finances, and health. Granted the financial aspect may be arranged by mutual agreement but there should never be an expectation that the other person is to "handle" any of those things for you. If you depend on someone else to make you feel worthy, loved, pay your bills, and handle your health for you, you will find yourself in quite a pickle should they tire of these tasks and move on. Not to mention, your self-confidence will be far higher if you choose to own these three things on your own, and then simply share life with your partner. Spend the time to find your own path for these things, and fully own them. Use these questions, both on yourself and with your partner, to help you.

CHAPTER 5

Apocalyptic Feelings

FORTY-TWO PERCENT OF PEOPLE WHO COMMIT SUICIDE ALLEGEDLY do so due to relationship issues. Why? Seven billion people on the planet and we humans are willing to kill ourselves if ONE does not like us or treat us the way we think they should. Why is that? Anyone who has been through the pain of a bad relationship, or a bad breakup has likely experienced some level of intense triggers. Do you feel like, at that point, you are empty and numb? Like you have no future? Like there is nothing left worth living for. Is that true? No, of course not. It is ridiculous to presume there is only one right fit for you on this planet teeming with humanity. So why on earth do we feel this way?

The feelings we have when we are deep in a relationship are not always about love for the other person or even the other person's love for us. It is much more internalized. What does this mean?

First, we tend to bundle up our personal hopes, dreams and fantasies and drape them over our significant other for completion. Think hard about someone you fell in love with. Why did you fall in love with them? If they were attractive, could it be that being with them made you feel more worthy and attractive? If so, that is about your needs, not your selfless love for them. If they were smart, did it mean they made you proud in social settings? Did it make you feel they would earn a good living and create the lifestyle you desired? How often do we see women marry for this reason and the relationship fall apart the moment the woman achieves her own success? The fact is, once you understand where your feelings come from, and connect with your own deepest personal hopes and dreams so that you can potentially achieve those needs on your own, your relationship triggers will diminish. Selfless, true love rarely involves triggers. Once you have developed this ability, a breakup will invoke appropriate sadness, but it will not cause feelings of panic, desperation, anger, or fear. The goal is to grow to a place where you no longer feel you need or must get love. A place where you are full inside, you are overflowing, and you are ready to share some of that bounty with an equally complete partner.

Second, many of our reactions in "love" are based on love survival maps we learned in early childhood. As children our very survival depended on a caregiver loving us. It was literally life or death. We learned to adapt to doing whatever was needed to guarantee their attention. This survival instinct still shapes our behavior as adults, resulting in a host of fears and actions related to rejection, inadequacy, or abandonment. As babies, we looked at our parents' faces and interpreted their expressions to determine our own self-worth. The flaw here is that their expressions of fear or anxiety may have had nothing to do with us and everything to do with their stressors or inadequacies. Yet, we interpreted those expressions as identifying our self-worth. We developed early coping skills to ensure that we received quick fix doses of safety and love hormones like oxytocin in any way possible. We adapted by developing traits of narcissism or codependency or other coping strategies to obtain the best responses from them so we could "make it." This was good in the sense that it helped us survive childhood.

As adults though, we are fully capable of being our own caregivers.

Gaining the love of others no longer must dictate our survival. In fact, it can be the cherry on top of an already full happy life. Once we can fill our own cup, relationships no longer define or control us, they simply enhance us.

As we work to fill our own cup, we can also work to let go of the need to control other people's cups. We waste unbelievable amounts of energy internalizing other people's crappy actions. When someone cheats on us or leaves us rather than put in the effort to build the relationship, sometimes we spend hours letting that incident destroy our self-worth. Our ego wants to engage in guilt, shame, blame, and "what ifs." It wants to tell us ridiculous lies, like, "If you had been prettier or done more of what he wanted, he or she wouldn't have left." The truth is this: Most choices people make have very little to do with us and very much to do with internal forces driving them. Most of which we have zero control over. Let it be. Let them do what they'll do. We can only control ourselves.

My friend Jamie was a great example of this. She had dated a great guy for almost a year. Things seemed perfect. She knew he was on the verge of proposing. One week she went on a trip with her college class for a school performance. On the trip, the group began drinking and she openly made out with another guy. Several of their classmates saw it. News, of course, made it back to her boyfriend. He was devastated. He was so hurt, he never even reached out to her. He literally disappeared. She really did not even know why she had done what she did, so she had nothing to say about it. Yet she did not apologize. They both simply walked away. Although they never spoke again, for years he blamed himself, questioning repeatedly why he was not enough, what he had done wrong, why he did not measure up. He suffered depression and lack of motivation for months. All that emotional exhaustion was for nothing because none of it was true.

The truth, and underlying cause, although she did not understand it for decades to come, was that she had a huge fear of commitment. Unless we are highly self-aware, our minds do not make behavioral decisions for us. Our deep core emotions do. In her case, her core traits or priorities at that time were independence and autonomy and new challenges. None of which aligned with settling down to suburban baby-making. As a result, almost without her even knowing, her deep core chose to take action to make sure her path aligned with her traits. Had she been emotionally evolved and self-aware, she could have recognized her inner anxiety regarding an impending proposal and worked through it, honoring her feelings, and making an informed decision. Had she done that, she would have then talked through her feelings in a respectful way with him, and they could have jointly decided how to proceed.

The moral of the story for the guy in this example is this: Do not let other people's baggage define your own self-worth. Although it is always important to do self-analysis and see how you can improve yourself, engaging in shame, blame, guilt, what-if game is generally based on untruths and is a waste of energy. Control yourself. Relinquish control of others.

Often when we feel most triggered by a partner is when we feel dependent on them for a certain need. It may be safety, financial support, connection, affection, or validation that you have an expectation the other person "owes" you. The thing to remember is this: You should never have to feel fully dependent on someone else for any of these things. You can enjoy sharing these things with others. You can purposely choose interdependence. But fully depending on someone for any of these items leads to frustration and impossible expectations. Why? Because no one is going to be able to fully know, and meet, your innermost needs all the time. Even your parents, even if they were good parents, could not do that. It is your job.

Rather than give your power to another person by feeling dependent and, consequently, frustrated, develop independence in yourself and your higher power and then share interdependence with someone else. If the other person fails to meet your expectations of interdependence, set a boundary. If they are unable to meet your boundary, be able to walk away. The next time you feel extremely triggered by a partner, ask yourself what need of yours you are relying on them for, and whether you can meet that need yourself. If so, work on that. This will keep you from feeling so emotionally reactive. You will be more able to make rational decisions about what you are and are not willing to tolerate in the relationship.

When our emotions are in control, they often lead us into brick walls. Sometimes, however, they help us instantly lunge out of the way when a tiger is leaping at us! They are a critical aspect of our survival, but they must be managed, so that we do not spend our whole lives acting like toddlers whenever we feel triggered.

When we feel hurt, our brain often tells us the lie that the only way to feel better is to force, control, and make the other person do what we want them to. This is ego. This is untrue. It is also virtually impossible to have a healthy relationship when we are continually manipulating the other person to adapt to our every feeling, need and whim. You may not think you are trying to "control" the other person but sometimes even being overly nice or accommodating can be a method of control. Think carefully about whether your actions are done purely out of love or to cause that person to act toward you in a certain way. If the latter, you are engaged in manipulation. Try honest communication about your feelings instead.

If manipulation and control of others is not your sole option to feel better, what are the other ways? There are so many. One way is to bring a value add to the equation yourself. Another way is honest, non-judgmental communication. Yet another way is to set boundaries. All of these require courage and discipline. Finger pointing and manipulating require neither because they are the default ego-driven way.

Let's look at some examples:

Isaac wants to go golfing (or shopping or running or fill in the blank) all day on Saturday.

His wife Jessica has no plans and immediately feels triggered, knowing she will be alone and likely bored all day.

A self-absorbed ego driven reaction could manifest as any of the following:

- ❖ Sulking.
- ❖ Pointing fingers "You never spend time with me, you always make me last priority."
- ❖ Manipulating by bribing or being seductive to make Isaac stay.
- ❖ Controlling by issuing a command to stay or ultimatum.

A loving, empathetic reaction could manifest like this:

- ❖ Jessica quietly acknowledges their trigger and breathes, letting the feeling pass.
  - ○ Jessica then gives a moment of reflection, "Isaac has friends and hobbies. This is healthy. Perhaps I should as well. This could be fun. Let me work on this today." Jessica now has a plan and is no longer triggered, able to sincerely be happy for Isaac to go enjoy his day. Or,

o   Another healthy possibility is that Jessica says, "I sometimes feel lonely when you are gone all day. I don't want you to feel like you must stay for that reason. I am simply sharing how I feel." This honest vulnerability opens the door for collaborative communication where both parties work on ways to make the scenario better.

o   If Isaac reacts to Jessica's second response negatively, such as, "I don't care what you think, I'm going to go play golf whenever I want," this could be a sign that Jessica needs to set a boundary and be willing to walk away from the relationship if Jessica's feelings are habitually disregarded.

Notice that all the empathetic reactions restore control of the situation and the feelings to Jessica. It was Jessica's trigger originally. Therefore, it is Jessica's responsibility to resolve her own feelings in a mature and communicative way. Think about how a 4-year-old would react to this situation? Are they likely to engage in the ego driven first 4 behaviors? Of course, they are. As we mature, we want to progress from this easy reactive state to one that is thoughtful and purposeful, one that builds relationships and builds self-confidence.

The truth is, if Jessica can thoughtfully respond in the second manner, she will feel empowered, strong, and confident. If Jessica responds in an ego-driven manner, Jessica will feel victimized, drained and resentful. Jessica is in control and her self-worth depends upon how she chooses to respond and react.

Learning healthy interdependence is key to a strong relationship. But what if the relationship falls apart? How do you handle it? It's normal to have to ride a pendulum of feelings after a brutal fight or at the end of a relationship. First, you'll want to blame them for everything. Later you may blame yourself for everything. Neither is true. Be patient with yourself and know that in the long run you will come to a place of greater understanding where you'll realize it was likely a mix of both and many other factors, some of which were probably never in your control at all. Our ego naturally will take us on a ride from self-righteous to self-loathing as we work toward a place of empathy and collaboration.

Some people, however, never get over their past relationships. They live for years weighed down by a swirling mire of confusing thoughts and feelings, never quite able to fully enjoy the present because of continually living in the past and what might have been. Women are more prone to this than men. For biological reasons, women are hard wired to seek connection and then fight for it to last. For the sake of survival of children and family units, our souls seek to hold tight, sometimes even when we shouldn't. We also seek to fix, to nurture, to heal. All of these are good traits, and can also be found in men, but sometimes our hard-wired traits do not serve us well.

These are the same traits that often cause high performing, high achieving independent women to be drawn to underperforming, attention seeking men. These kinds of men are often prone to addictions and excess neediness. Their temperament makes this type of woman feel powerful and needed, but also slowly drains the life from her. No matter how destructive this dynamic becomes, the risk is that the woman will stay, because she is biologically hard wired to do so. She intuitively wants to figure out the problem, solve the issues, and make everything work.

How many times have you seen the above scenario played out? Relationship addiction feels like noble work, perhaps even loyalty, but it is, in fact, simply addiction. Recognizing that is the first step for these women (or men) to regain their lives, thoughts, and emotions.

How do you know if you are obsessing over the past or falling prey to relationship addiction?

Do you find yourself replaying what you think you did wrong and thinking if you could only change this or that, you would still have the relationship?

Do you glamorize the past? Often relationships that were miserable while we were in them seem suddenly magical when viewed from the rearview mirror. This is an illusion. Chalk it up to mermaids and unicorns and let that wistful feeling go.

Are you often distracted by memories or thoughts of past relationships? To the point that you cannot concentrate on new projects or events. Does that feel like quicksand that is holding you back? Does it feel like a puzzle you need to solve, but can't quite figure out how to?

Do you mindlessly scroll online, with an empty feeling, hoping to stumble on some answer or closure to how you feel? As if you will somehow find that missing link on your phone? The clue or secret that will make it all make sense.

Do you sometimes feel an insatiable urge to "talk through things" one more time with that person? Do you tell yourself it is for closure or some other legitimate sounding excuse?

Do you now justify all the things the other person did that, at the time, you felt were intolerable?

If you find yourself doing these things, do some online research on how to overcome relationship addiction, or consider talking to a therapist. Life is far too short to fall victim to an addiction and not even realize that is what you have done.

Sometimes the painful circumstances of a closed door are the universe's way of extracting us from a situation we should not be in. Have you ever experienced this? I can think of so many times I wanted a certain relationship or job or circumstance so badly and yet, years later I was phenomenally grateful it did not work out. What felt so devastating at the time was, in fact, a blessing and later enabled much better opportunities. Think back through your life and see if you can identify memories of events that showcase this. Take a moment to thank the universe for all the times it helped you dodge a bullet.

Although experiencing intense trauma, such as from a painful relationship break-up, can be incredibly painful and scary, it also, ironically, can be a great path toward insight, creativity, and intuition. After I went through intense trauma related to multiple deaths, within months of each other, of a few close family members and friends. I put considerable energy into therapy from a mental health professional, journaling, meditation, and yoga. Although painful, it also came to be one of the most insightful periods of my life. I viewed daily life differently. My intuition became very heightened. I felt much more spiritually in touch. It was like being a child and rediscovering the world. Every experience and emotion are part of our life journey. Explore them all.

CHAPTER 6

Forging a Way
Out of Limbo

NOT LONG AGO I HAD A CONVERSATION WITH A FRIEND IN HIS mid-seventies. He is wealthy, brilliant, a pillar of his community and has been married for over thirty years. By all appearances, he is the epitome of success. We talked about how challenging relationships can be and how much emotional growth it takes to be a solid partner, a deep partner. The floodgates then opened. He began telling me how he had been lonely and miserable in his marriage for decades. How he says little, to keep the peace. How he cannot leave due to the financial ramifications and the social stigma. He feels responsible to stay with her. He loves her. But he is miserable. He fights a mental battle every day. Should I stay or should I go? Life is too short to stay. But it will cause so much conflict and controversy to go. In his head, the same daily words swirled incessantly.

Is it worth it? What will she do? Will she self-destruct and blame me? Will I end up as the bad guy? What will my friends say? What will her friends say?

My friend was a good person who wanted to be loyal and do the right thing but he was tired of walking on eggshells and not having a supportive partner. What was the answer? Unfortunately for him, (and for her) he surrendered. He gave up. He emotionally threw in the towel and chose to simply exist, trapped on a treadmill of mediocrity till one or both of them pass from this life.

This is the ultimate tragedy: To be trapped in a state of being that you are not emotionally engaged with. With someone who doesn't get you and who you don't get. Or in a lifestyle that isn't your authentic self. To be trapped in a mutual place of misunderstanding and chronic discontent. Is there any worse way to live?

And yet, the tweaks that would be needed to bring my friend's isolated, soul-sucking marriage to a place of fun and joy were not all that complicated. They would start with each person clearing their own emotional baggage, recognizing their own blinders, and taking responsibility. Whether that process ended in a needed conscious uncoupling or in a roadmap to soulmate happiness, either would be preferable to the uncertain trauma of being in limbo. It mattered less which route he chose and mattered far more that he chose one path and fully committed to it, to live with courage and authenticity.

It is important to pick a path and follow it with your whole heart. It is about being brutally honest with yourself and highly purposeful in your communications and actions with others. It is about doing what you need to do to feel full, authentic, and creative.

In the pages that follow, you will find stories that will help you pick paths for all the roads of your life, including relationships. You will discover ways to change the way you handle your workplace, your teenagers, your friendships and, most importantly, your dreams. The processes in this book will help you shed emotional suitcases, kick out the unwanted tenants living on free rent in your mind, and calm your soul. You will remember what it feels like to be creative, to be motivated, to be psyched up about life. It's a process that leads to a truly intoxicating life, that also inspires others.

Chronic Discontent

Have you ever met someone who is chronically discontented?

Someone who manages to find a way to always blame their unhappiness on someone or something else. Their partners, jobs, cities, situations, and lives change, **yet their outlook remains the same.** These are the people, maybe even you, who spend critical chunks of time in their current relationship dwelling on their last relationship or fantasizing about a future one. They compare, contrast, and find themselves in an overthinking quagmire of recurrent non-bliss. They are constantly thinking "what-if?"

What if this person I'm with dressed better or made more money?

Or did their share of the housework? Then I'd be happy!

What if I had a better job or my boss were nicer, or I were skinnier? Then I'd be happy!

What if my child got better grades or was more respectful or acted more loving?

The "what-if" game is like the limbo game. It is the "go to Jail" card in Monopoly. It is the place you should never find yourself and if you do, you should exit as quickly as possible. There is no rainbow and no happy ending in the "what-if" game or the over-thinking indecisive limbo game.

This type of thinking comes from our wounded child self. As we evolve into our higher self, we learn to simply accept where we are in this moment, to stop trying to control and change it, but to merely take it in, learn from it, appreciate, and understand it. We learn to self-soothe and set calm boundaries, while being curious and interested in the people and situations around us. We stop feeling threatened and thereby stop trying to escape to the past or future. We learn to be. Here. Now. This is the place where true happiness is found because this present moment, this place right now, is truly all we have. We can't travel back in time, and we may not see another day. So, take one moment and look around. Breathe deep.

What do you see? Smell? Taste? Feel? What can you find to love about this moment right now? Are you safe? Full? Comfortable? Loved by someone?

There is one day that is more vividly etched into my brain than any other day in my life. It was the day of my 4th birthday, and it is the earliest memory I have. I had a troubled childhood but on the day of my 4th birthday, something amazing happened. My normally angry and impatient father, who did not believe in birthdays, decided on a whim to cook hotdogs, and cut a fresh watermelon for my birthday. It was the only day in my entire life I ever remember him noticing me, with no agenda. I remember it like it was yesterday. I stood on the back porch, gazed out over the backyard, and thought to myself, "Today I am 4. I will never again be 4. I want to remember every moment of this day and see if I can remember it when I'm old." It was such an old soul thing to think and to say to myself. And yet, I do remember. I remember every inch of that backyard scene. I remember Dad seeming happy for one of the only times in my life. I remember the hotdogs. I remember the thought distinctly. On that day, in that moment, my 4-year-old inner self understood more than I ever have since, how to be fully and truly present. I felt more connected to my inner self and my source on that day than I ever have in my life. This memory brings me phenomenal happiness, for reasons I cannot explain. I want more of these deeply etched moments and memories. All I must do is be deeply present, aware, and purposeful about creating these memories.

Chronic discontent leads to limbo because although the person knows they are unhappy, deep down inside their subconscious they recognize that changing circumstances is not the key. Consciously the person thinks they should get a divorce or change jobs or move and they will be happy. Subconsciously though, they recognize that the source of true discontent is never situational, it is abandonment of self. So, they are caught in a constant tug of war between wanting to leave the situation and yet realizing the real answer is usually to stay. The real answer is to first change what is inside. To change what is inside requires connecting with oneself and becoming very present.

We as humans can be happy in almost any situation, short of actual abuse. Joy and happiness are a state of mind, a place of inner content. Ironically, because our outer world almost always mirrors our inner world, once we find that place of inner content, our exterior situational world slowly begins to adapt to match. We begin to manifest all the exterior things we once sought, once we first align with the right energy on the inside. The wrong people begin to drift away. The right people become attracted to us. The right job finds us. Things begin to fall into place. The work to make this happen, all happens on the inside.

Are you ready for action step number one? It will sound ridiculous. If you are ready for big changes in your life, trust the process. Here is step one.

Lay on your left side. Put your right hand under your left ribs, up high. Hold your heartbeat in your hand. Close your eyes. Really feel each pulsation. Each contraction. This is your heart, beating to flow blood through every inch of your body. It's yours, only yours. It's you. The innermost you. The most important part of you. This is connecting with you. Being present with you. Feeling the most alive part of you. Talk to your heart.

Say "I love you. I feel you. I am going to give you the best life. We are going to find joy and curiosity in everything. You are mine and I will cherish you. I will take the best care of our body to support you. Together we will take the best care of others by always choosing to ask questions rather than to judge. To listen rather than lecture. I feel you."

Few people are connected to themselves. They are a brain, perched as a silo on top of a body, lost in thoughts of past and future, haunted by guilt, anger, fear, shame, and anxiety, forgetting the power of their beating, pulsating, living heart. To feel full and to have certainty, we must find ways to reconnect our mind, body, heart, and soul.

The more you can train yourself to connect to your heart and to be fully engaged in the present moment, the more you will find it shockingly easy to make decisions and to say exactly the right words in difficult situations. Rather than being confused by monkey brain and over-thinking, you will allow your intuition to be more assertive. The words, decisions and actions will flow from you effortlessly. This is the purpose behind meditation as well. There is a reason most ultra-successful career leaders incorporate meditation into their lives. Exercises like the heartbeat exercise and meditation connect you to your inner self which enables you to clear the haze and effortlessly see the right paths. You will stop over-thinking and start feeling exactly what you need to do. As you learn to do this, you will exit the limbo of chronic discontent and clearly see how to walk the paths ahead of you.

We talked in chapter 2 about your "Thing." Think about your Thing for a minute. Can you use this exercise to help conquer the Thing?

Goodbye limbo. Hello clarity, certainty, and confidence.

CHAPTER 7

Spin It Till You Win It

What Does it Mean to Manifest?

WHY DOES IT SEEM THAT SOME PEOPLE ALWAYS WIN? NO MATTER what challenges they face in life, they always seem to come out on top?

The book *The Brain Mechanic* by Spencer Lord teaches the concept that our feelings are largely created not by our situations, but rather by the story we tell ourselves about our situations. Similarly, in murder investigations, eyewitness accounts often vary wildly. Why? Because the way we see the world differs a lot based on our individual thought patterns.

People say our external world is merely a mirror of our internal world, which is why we can manifest the circumstances we desire, once we learn to better manage our internal thoughts and stories. Is this true? Let's look.

Joey and Anna had been happily married for over 10 years when things started going south. Anna had received a huge promotion that required a cross country move. Thrilled, she threw herself into work. Joey, because of the move, found himself much less busy as he was able to almost retire. Left alone for many hours of the day, he became consumed in the looping thoughts of his own mind.

His greatest fear had always been abandonment, and he had secretly always feared that Anna would leave him for someone else. Before the move, when he had been busy and fulfilled with work, he thought about it rarely. Now he thought about it daily. Soon, her every word and action began to strike him as a red flag. Signs of her fading interest.

Frustrated and fearful, he began acting out. Frustrated by his immature behavior, Anna began withdrawing. One day, he filed for divorce. She never quite understood why he did it, but she couldn't talk him out of it.

Years later, they talked.

"Why did you leave," she asked? We never really fought, we had some communication issues, but we could have easily worked those out with help.

"You despised me," he said, looking at her in surprise, not understanding how she could miss the obvious reason.

"What?" She said confused. I loved you. I was frustrated by some of your behavior toward the end, but I never despised you as a person. He didn't believe her.

Joey and Anna's story is a classic example of an unproductive story. In Joey's state of mind, he perceived everything far more dramatically than it was. When she worked late, he told himself she didn't want to spend time with him. When she rushed out to work in the mornings and forgot to kiss him goodbye, he told himself she no longer found him attractive. When her text replies to him during the day were curt, he told himself she no longer cared about him. Over time, he crafted a story that she despised him. This story crushed his self-confidence and made him feel scared, alone, and angry. With that story in hand, his brain quickly reverted to the times as a child he felt neglected and abandoned by his mother. It was a familiar place, painful but comfortable. With this narrative, he found himself once again to be the victim. As a small child, he had no control over his situation with his mother. His brain therefore concluded he similarly had no control over the situation with his wife. With this self-created position of powerlessness, he had no accountability or responsibility. He could sadly chalk the situation up to her despising him, leave because he saw himself as powerless and use his story to try to go gain the sympathy and love of other women.

Anna's perspective, however, was far different. She loved Joey. She felt the same about him she always had. When she worked late it was because she was determined not to fail at the job that caused them to have to move across the country. She didn't want to let her or Joey down. When she rushed out to work in the mornings, it was because her mind was spinning with ideas. High on adrenaline, she knew if she stopped to cuddle in bed, she'd lose her motivation and the mindset she needed to conquer the day. When she curtly replied to texts, she was simply trying to efficiently be responsive yet juggle her new job duties.

What if Joey had told himself a different story? What if his story had been, "Wow, I'm so lucky. I have a hardworking and smart wife and because of her I can practically retire already. That means I can go ahead and start following my passions and dreams. I can't wait to work on these ideas and share them with her! We're going to have an amazing future!"

When they saw each other at the end of the day, Joey would have been interesting and exciting to be around. He would have been thrilled to see her and she would have responded similarly. Instead, because of his story, he acted fearful and resentful which began causing Anna to doubt him and their relationship. The cycle snowballed, causing them both to lose trust and confidence in each other. The result of this one changed story would have been wildly different.

Our thoughts do become things. Our outer world is, yes, to a large degree, created by our inner world. This is what it means to manifest.

How Do You Spin it Till You Win It?

Sometimes you do have to fake it till you make it, or, more accurately spin that story till you win that outcome. It is in your best interest to look at various stories that could fit the situation you are in and then pick the one that serves you best. In Joey's example, it is clear which story would have led to the best outcome for him.

3 Ways to Spin it Till You Win It:

1) For every situation you are in, identify the feeling you are having. Next, ask yourself what story you are telling yourself that is causing that feeling.
2) Then, ask yourself what other stories might possibly also be accurate. Find stories that will serve you and others the most.
3) then spin that story until it is as positive and useful as it can be!

Once you pick the winning story, hold it tight! Here's the reality. Let's say Joey's first story had been "right." Let's say Anna really was starting to fall out of love with him.

Which story could have changed that scenario? Certainly not the one he picked.

If you want to win, for every situation pick a winning story, then spin it till you win it.

Everyone wants confidence and many think they do not take risks because of their lack of confidence.

The trick is this: Confidence does not lead to doing bigger things. Taking risks to do bigger things while we are fearful leads to confidence. Actions are the way.

For any given situation, there are a variety of plausible stories you can apply to the event. The one you select will determine how you feel about the event, and, in turn, determine your outlook, demeanor and often, your success.

Let's try some real-life examples:

My friend's teenage daughter was headed to a job interview. She said she was extremely nervous, almost to the point of a panic attack. I asked her, "What is the story you have told yourself about this interview?" She looked puzzled. I repeated myself. What is the meaning to you of this job? What is its importance? What is the story surrounding it? She said, "Well, I am very unhappy in my current job because my boss is very difficult. I must get this new job so I can get out of the old one. I can't take another day there!" My response: "It sounds as though you have pinned your happiness on an outcome. That will always cause anxiety. We cannot control every outcome. Even if you are perfect in the interview, other factors may cause them to not give you the job. Not all aspects of this are under your control. Therefore, let's frame a more realistic story. How about this. 'I would really like to land this job. Therefore, I am going to find my calm focused center so I can do my best in the interview. I will trust the universe that it may not be the best path, and, in fact, it is possible that my best path for my future may be in staying in my current job to learn how to effectively navigate difficult people. I accept either outcome. Regardless, I will shine in my interview and not be concerned with the outcome.'" Now you have created a story well within your control. The anxiety subsides. Your body settles. You are focused and ready to go do your best.

Here's another example: You are late to work, frazzled and upset. You feel anxious and angry. You realize the narrative playing in your mind is "I am always late; I need to get myself together. I hate this job. Why does it start so early? And why do the kids always keep me up so late. I can't handle this!!" You recognize this and stop to reframe the narrative to this. "Yikes, I'm running a bit late. It's ok, I'll talk to my boss when I get there. Since I don't like the feeling of being late, I am going to set some parameters in my life with alarms and going to bed earlier so this doesn't happen again. Let me put a reminder on my phone to work on that tonight. I'm proud of myself for recognizing my pattern of lateness and fixing this for the future." The feelings of anxiety and anger melt away. You walk into work 10 min late but collected. You thank your boss for being patient with you and state that you are putting some parameters in place, so it does not happen again. You proceed with your workday.

Here's a third: You arrive home, and the house is a mess. Your spouse is sitting on the couch playing on their phone. You have had a long day. You instantly feel resentment, anger, frustration flood you. Why? The story you are likely telling yourself is this: "I deserve better than this. Why am I the one who must do everything? I work so hard. I'm so tired. I can't keep doing this.' This story will make you feel terrible inside and will cause you to lash out at your significant other. Here's a rewrite: "Whoa, the house is a mess. And Joe /Josie is sitting there on the phone. Wonder what's up with that? Well, I'm tired. I am not going to overwhelm myself with tackling this or starting a fight right now. I'm going to change into something comfortable, eat some food and then talk to them. When I talk to them, I'm going to say this: "Hey are you doing ok? You seem lost in your phone. What's up? I know you know it makes me feel anxious when the house is a wreck. I'm feeling that anxiety now. Would you be willing to help clean it up with me?"

The story we tell ourselves is everything. It controls how we think, feel, act, speak and behave. It controls what type of energy we draw toward us and how we react in every situation. It is the master key, and you are 100% in charge of it.

Here's another example, albeit a silly one. Recently I went snowboarding with my daughters. They learned young and quickly far surpassed my abilities. Because I learned later in life, and because I only go sporadically, I am always nervous about exiting the ski lift and always nervous about the first few runs. A few months prior, I had gone to Tahoe with friends and had a delightful time. Because I was so excited, I immediately booked a follow up trip. This second trip, everything went wrong. For some reason, I kept dwelling on whether I might fall exiting the chair. Whatever we focus on can become our truth and in this case it did. I fell hard upon exiting the ski lift chair and seriously hurt my lower back. I had never done this before. Because my back was so injured, I was unable to snowboard the rest of the day. I was demoralized, sad, frustrated. My mind went to a dark place. I soon began having thoughts that I was too old for such an aggressive sport, that I wasn't coordinated, that I would never have the requisite balance and skill. This evolved into thoughts that perhaps my days of adrenaline sports were behind me. That I was doomed to a future of "safe" hobbies. This in turn meandered its way into dark thoughts that I would no longer be fun, and my daughters would no longer want to go on trips with me. In fact, my boyfriend probably would not either. Ahh how the story runs away with us and unnecessarily leads us down a rabbit hole of morose. By the end of my self-imposed pity party, I felt old, tired, useless, and drained. And then I realized something. Although this story could be true, it did not have to be true. It was simply one story, one version of many other possibilities.

Out of curiosity, I googled "snowboarding when older". I found story upon story of people in the 50's, 60's, 70's and beyond tearing up the slopes. I found myself smiling and loving these stories. I began to reconstruct what happened that day and was able to identify why I fell. First, I had made the mistake of boarding the ski lift with the fear of falling heavily on my mind. If you are riding a bike and you stare at a pothole in the road you will ride right into it. My fall was no different. It was a result of my negative obsession manifested. In addition, I realized my positioning when I left the seat was wrong. I also realized that I, because of my limited skill, need to always start on green slopes to "find my sea legs" before moving on to more difficult slopes. In this case I went straight to a hard blue and allowed my fear to psyche me out. I made a plan for what to do next time. I also reminded myself that my worth to my daughters was certainly not based on my sports ability. They likely would not abandon me over my snowboarding skills. I changed my whole story narrative. My new narrative was that, yes, I had one bad day, but I would go into my next trip with the mindset of gracefully exiting the chair lift, not with the fear of falling. The rest of the trip I was happy and fine.

Any time and every time you are feeling uncomfortable emotions, stop, look in the mirror and ask yourself what the narrative playing in your brain is. If it is not a productive narrative, pick a different story.

CHAPTER 8

Well, Hello,
Shadow Side

OUR IDENTITY IS A PRODUCT OF ALL OUR FEELINGS, INCLUDING our uncomfortable ones. When we deny our negative feelings, we, in turn, also deny our positive ones. We must acknowledge ALL of them, to fully feel ANY of them. Similarly, when we diminish or "talk someone out of" their uncomfortable feelings, we are denying their experience.

In Jungian psychology, the shadow side is either an unconscious aspect of the personality that the conscious mind ego does not identify, or the entirety of the unconscious, meaning the parts of you that you are not aware of or do not want to acknowledge. Because we tend to reject or choose to remain ignorant of what we consider to be the least desirable parts of our personality, the shadow is often largely negative. These parts of us are still, however, parts of us. If we do not acknowledge them, they rule us in other ways.

Often, we are attracted to those who exhibit parts of our shadow side. For example, if we are hyper-disciplined, organized and task-oriented, often we are highly attracted to someone who is laid back and fun-loving. Because those are parts of ourselves we have pushed down and rejected, we are attracted to someone who experiences what we have not allowed ourselves to experience. This is exciting at first, but over the years can become a point of contention in the relationship if both partners strive to force the other person to be more like themselves.

The real goal is to get to know all the parts of us, especially our shadow side. Our triggers can be a great place to start. Sometimes this is a difficult thing to do on our own. A great exercise is to do it with someone else.

When someone shares with you that they are feeling a particular way, it is a huge opportunity to explore who they are, with them. Uncomfortable feelings are a roadmap for keeping us true to our authentic self. They need to be explored with curiosity and excitement.

If this person touched a hot stove, you wouldn't try to talk them out of their pain. You wouldn't say "Now, hon, just be happy, focus on how the rest of your body is unburned; it wasn't that big of a burn, it shouldn't feel that bad, go play and take your mind off it."

Of course not! You would say, "Oh wow! I bet that hurt! Let's look closely at the burn. Where does it hurt? How did it happen? Let's figure out what makes it feel better. I'm so proud of how well you're handling the pain. You're amazing!"

See the difference? One response is diminishing and the other is empowering.

This is what we want to do when others experience intense emotions, and we also want to do it for ourselves. Go deep. Go explore. Pull back the layers. See what you find. This is how intimacy and trust are created.

Why is our tendency to minimize and dismiss grief, anxiety, sadness, anger, fear, or resentment, while fully acknowledging cancer, diabetes, and heart disease?

I would argue the former are far more worthy of our exploration, as delving into those layers helps unearth all the parts of a person's identity and, more importantly, their gifts to the world, as we found in the Triggers Method.

CASE STUDY

Recently, a young woman, Emma, dealt with a situation that could have ended in a heartbreak. She called late at night with the following real encounter, concerning her relationship with her husband, Doug:

Emma: I'm in bed dying slowly. I thought I was cool but now having more problems. What's wrong with me?

Supporter: Aww, maybe you need sleep? Food? Do you want to talk?

Emma: I feel so weird about life lately. I guess that comes with being twenty-five. I hate Doug so much. I don't even care anymore.

Supporter: That's not true. You may feel triggered by him. And that's OK. Maybe some sleep would be best right now? You've had a lot of stress today.

Emma: I told him I hate him, and I've always meant it. He pushes me to that point in my most vulnerable times. He can suffer for all I care. He is incapable of support. Because it's his big day, his birthday. And he thinks I'm acting out.

Supporter: You may feel that way right now ... but that feeling will pass and those are words that should never be said to any person. I understand that you feel very upset, and that's understandable, but I don't want you to say things you'll regret later. Much better that you vent to me than him when you feel this upset.

Emma: I ended things, locked the door, and made him sleep on the couch.

Supporter: That is not resolving anything. That is your ego running away with your life. This makes me very sad for both of you.

Emma: Yeah well, so does Mr. Zero Mistakes and Perfect. No matter how slowly and calmly I tell him anything, his alter ego comes out. I'm freakin' done.

Supporter: Do you feel better now?

Emma: Nooooooo.

Supporter: Exactly.

Emma: It's not my fault he's dumb. And rude. I'm not a slave with a smile, for his reputation.

Supporter: So you get to be right. And alone. Is that what you want?

Emma: I'm fine with being alone if I'm not being controlled.

Supporter: How would you feel if it were your birthday, and you were in his shoes? And he was deep in his own issues and wanted nothing to do with your birthday? I'm not defending him. Just hoping to give you both perspectives.

Emma: He doesn't have any of his own issues. He uses mine. And even if he did, I'd leave him be and not provoke him. But he had to

prove me. I guess I'm tired of letting people walk on me and if that's
what his nature is, I don't think I'm ready to be that. I'm destroyed. I
don't care. I tried to be calm, but I can't be Wonder Woman.

Supporter: It sounds like you basically took all your childhood
triggers and dumped them on him. He may have triggered this, but
he did not cause these deep feelings you have. Those emotions are
yours to work through, not his. I say this while feeling the greatest
empathy because I do get it.

Emma: But how many times does that have to happen? I give up. I've
always regretted saying these things before but now I don't because I
feel that my heart is legit.

Supporter: Maybe a million times more. Loving someone means you
don't keep score. You expect there to be battles and you work through
them.

Emma: My heart is tired of not being understood or being able to
communicate with him in our times of need.

Supporter: I understand.

Emma: That's more than compromise and it's hard to love him.
Always has been. Nothing I do is ever enough for him.

Supporter: But ... I'm going to be very blunt with you. He is not ever
going to fully understand your emotions. They are YOUR emotions.
It is your job to work through them. Not his. Could he be more
compassionate? Sure. But either way you must not rely on him to fix
those when you are having a hard time.

Emma: I don't expect much, trust me. But I always get more grief
when I am vulnerable.

Supporter: The universe is funny. It often pairs us with a person who triggers our old wounds, so we are forced to face them and do the work. Doug's personality retriggers your very deep wounds. And I know that is excruciating.

Emma: What would you do?

Supporter: By acknowledging those deep wounds and loving yourself even more because of them, you are healing. It's about finding and facing our wounds and loving ourselves with such great tenderness and compassion that those wounds heal, and no one can ever trigger them again.

Your feelings matter. Immensely. Doug lacks the tools to help you when you need it most. Which likely makes him hugely frustrated that he can't fix it and so he takes that out on you. He does, however, hurt massively from your words and he doesn't know how to help. Let's try something.

Where do you feel the tension in your body right now?

Emma: In my heart.

Supporter: What does it feel like?

Emma: Like sad and scared and palpitating.

Supporter: Sad emoji face.

Emma: It feels overwhelming.

Supporter: Close your eyes. And picture your heart. Picture taking the best care of your heart. Wrapping a warm heavy blanket around it. Hugging it. Telling your heart that it is going to be OK. Because no matter what Doug ever does or doesn't do, Emma is going to take care of her heart. Just like a parent would for a child.

Spend at least five minutes with your eyes closed fully seeing and feeling and responding to your heart.

Emma: *long silence*

Emma: Thank you. I really needed this. I wish everyone could have you. I feel so at peace now.

Notice how in the beginning the supporter tried a variety of logic-based statements to try to reason with Emma. None particularly worked, although they gave Emma an opportunity to further share her feelings. The only intervention that truly worked was having Emma go deep into her physical body and acknowledge her feelings. One year later Emma is still happily married because she was able to effectively process her emotions and let them flow on.

Value Bomb: Be brave enough to get to know your shadow side and to help others get to know theirs. Fully acknowledging all your parts allows you to finally be whole.

CHAPTER 9

Secrets Kill (and So Do Narcissists)

WE CAN NEVER BE TRULY HAPPY IF WE HARBOR DARK SECRETS. Brené Brown has done incredible work in this area of shame and how it holds us back. The saying "the truth shall set you free" is, well, true. Most of us spend obscene amounts of time worrying about things we are hiding or afraid to say. We're afraid to tell our spouse we're upset they came home late. We're afraid to tell our child we love them fiercely and that the reason we sometimes micromanage them is that we don't want them to suffer pain or loss.

We worry and ruminate about a zillion things rather than just saying them. Find someone you can tell ANYTHING to, even if it is a counselor, and then do it. Release the weight of all your secret thoughts, your fears, your anxieties, your resentments, and your doubts. This is where you will find peace and reconnect with your creativity.

When we harbor our thoughts, they still come out. They come out as passive-aggressiveness, condescension, manipulation, sarcasm, anger and even violence. Find the right outlet where you can honor your voice and say what you need to say. I cannot underestimate the importance of this. Try to become self-aware of all the thoughts you "hide." Face them. Say them in a safe space, to a safe person. Release them. Having them spin circles in your head takes up precious mental energy you need for more fun things in life. You walking around stuck up in your head and looking morose gives the people you are with the insecure feeling that you are upset with them. This, even if untrue, causes spiderwebs of pain for others. Break the cycle.

The ultimate secret holder, and the ultimate left side of the ego scale, is the narcissist. The narcissist hides the very deep secret that they are not at all who they represent themselves to be. Inside they are frail, with low self-esteem, a terrible fear of rejection, and an inability to handle criticism. On the outside, what they portray, is a confident, charming, even cocky, persona.

What is a narcissist and why does it matter? All of us have some narcissistic traits and to some degree, this is healthy and good. A certain amount of narcissism is critical to developing and taking care of ourselves. Some level of narcissism is critical to accomplishing goals. Narcissism is key to our survival under certain circumstances. When narcissism becomes unhealthy is when it unnecessarily indulges our ego at the expense of others.

This all matters because emotional maturity is the gradual process of learning to substitute empathy for ego. A true narcissist is on the bottom rung of the ladder toward emotional maturity and is trying to knock off the people on the first and second rungs. This matters because knowledge is power. Your goal is to not be a narcissist and also to not be vulnerable to being knocked down by one.

The reason narcissists are so damaging is because of their deceptive charm and engulfing flattery. Because a true full-spectrum narcissist is 100 percent self-serving, they have no capacity for empathy or selfless love. Under normal circumstances, this would be obvious to a victim. To avoid revealing this, they must employ a high level of deceptive charm. This is the only way they can continue to "take" affection, attention, and validation from their victim, while committing to very little substance or accountability themselves. This charm is very confusing to the victim. It makes the victim think they are loved, which in turn guilts and excites them into loving back. Flattery is addicting. The problem is the victim is being slowly drained of life. They are throwing their love into a black bottomless hole. The narcissist can only take and leave. Come and go. They cannot provide sustained or substantive giving. They cannot and will not fight for you or support you except to the limited extent that it serves them. They will leave when things become difficult (when you can't give) and reemerge when you are healthy (and can give). Sometimes it will appear as though they are loving and supportive, which is more confusing. If you look closely, though, you will soon see that they only do this when they have an underlying self-serving goal.

You will not be able to progress on your own journey of emotional maturity if you are sucked into the abyss of serving a narcissist. Although it may feel like you are providing love and empathy, if you are entangled with a narcissist, whether it is in the form of a partner, a parent, a boss or even a friend, you are likely trapped in the thrill of intermittent reinforcement and the addiction of caretaking. You deserve better.

Rejection and intermittent reinforcement create obsession. Narcissists, consciously or not, use this to their advantage, to keep their victims always coming back, always reinventing themselves to get one more hit of the feeling when it's good. If you find yourself in this trap, seek professional help. Treat this as if it were the worst drug addiction. It is and can be just as deadly.

Think of it as a spectrum:

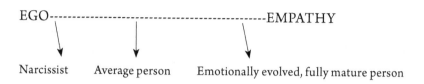

EGO--EMPATHY

Narcissist   Average person   Emotionally evolved, fully mature person

Our goal is to learn and grow and mature our way to the right side of the spectrum. It is there where we can fully serve others.

How do you know if you are a narcissist? One of the biggest issues with narcissists is they are unaware that is what they are. Their actions seem utterly justifiable to them. They cannot fathom why others are so sensitive and needy. Here is a quick quiz to see if you, or someone you know, might have narcissistic tendencies.

Do you sometimes feel superior to others and have fantasies of unlimited success, brilliance, power, beauty, or love?

Do you feel upset or wounded if someone else is the center of attention? Does it make you want to leave?

In a group, do you do most of the talking?

Do you find it hard to relate to people when they are overly emotional?

Do you often feel annoyed at the "neediness" of others?

Do you feel angry and reactive when someone criticizes you or tells you that you are wrong?

Does it feel annoying when others ask you for compromises or sacrifices?

Do you feel powerful when others compliment you or look up to you?

Do you often feel jealous of the success or lifestyle of others?

Do you cringe at the thought of an average or common life?

If you answered "yes" to many of these, it does not mean you are a diagnosable narcissist. It does mean you should do some research and investigate this more. Being a narcissist is not easy to self-diagnose and it can cause a world of harm to your loved ones. Care enough to consider the possibility that you may need to work in this arena.

Narcissism has the look of self-confidence but is borne of deeply fragile self-esteem. Narcissists can, at times, experience great pain, and they experience it because of scenarios most people would not find painful. For example, when they feel shunned by someone, or if they see a peer experiencing a success they want. They cannot handle criticism or rejection and therefore have a hard shell of "I don't care" façade to protect them. They are the ones doing the most talking in a group because they have a desperate need to be seen and valued. Narcissism has its roots in neglect and rejection. This does not mean their behavior should be excused away. Rather it should be faced and resolved.

Once a narcissist undergoes intensive therapy and finds the root of fragile self-esteem, they will find immense relief and a new-found peace and calm. The relentless anxiety and pursuit for more will relax, allowing them to be present, content and to give and receive love more fully. There is no greater gift, for themselves and for their loved ones.

Most importantly, once freed of their trapped insecurities, they will be able to focus on others and create meaningful legacy.

CHAPTER 10

Brain Inflammation, Impulsivity and Addiction

MANY SAY THAT WE HAVE BECOME AN INSTANT GRATIFICATION and an addiction-based society. What does this mean and how did this happen? One theory, and potentially partial explanation, has to do with brain inflammation. There have been numerous medical studies on the role brain inflammation can play in damaging the prefrontal cortex, leading to poor decision making, and the way in which repetitively engaging in self-indulgent activities (smoking, drinking, eating junk food) contributes to more brain inflammation. It quickly becomes a dangerous cycle.

In addition to brain inflammation, our world has made self-indulgence massively easy to engage in. In the past there were layers of discipline and accountability built around us. Lives had small doses of reward in return for extended periods of self-discipline. For example, you worked all day and relaxed at night. You worked all year and went on vacation maybe once a year. You were taught you had to do all your work before watching TV or playing. Now that has all changed. We have steady distraction and entertainment at our fingertips by virtue of our phones. We have constant accessibility to high sugar, high salt, high fat and carb processed foods. There are unlimited temptations available by our phones. We can get anything we want, on demand, with little required from us.

As a child growing up, I had a few alcoholics in the extended family. I remember recognizing early on that they were also, without exception, womanizers. I found that curious. Why did the two things seem to go hand in hand? They were all charming, fun men, who were terrible partners and parents. Why?

Now that I better understand science, it all makes more sense. Understanding the anatomy of the brain is key. The limbic part of the brain is located toward the center and is what keeps you alive. It wants to feel good; it dislikes pain, and it is essentially the "child" of your brain. It is what causes you to eat, to sleep, to seek out friendships and relationships, to do things that are fun, and to enjoy life. The prefrontal cortex is in your forehead area and plays the opposite role. It is the adult of your brain. It is your planning mechanism. It controls your emotional reactions, your decision making and your impulses. It helps you think before you act. It is what makes you a reliable partner and a responsible parent.

Substance abuse and addictions, ironically, affect the prefrontal cortex the most. It is quite unfortunate that the substance that will destroy your life will first target the area of your brain that would cause you to say no to it. Even non-chemical addictions, such as shopping, gambling, or sex, have this same effect of first short-circuiting will-power. This is also why a drunk person truly believes they are perfectly fine to drive. They lack insight and judgment due to the alcohol's mechanism of turning part of the brain off.

The American Society of Addiction Medicine defines it like this.

"Addiction is a primary, chronic disease of brain reward, motivation, memory and related circuitry. Dysfunction in these circuits leads to characteristic biological, psychological, social and spiritual manifestations. This is reflected in an individual pathologically pursuing reward and/or relief by substance use and other behaviors."

Let's think about this for a second. This does not only refer to the addict seeking drugs. It also refers to the codependent who is addicted to figuring out and solving the addict's disease process, rather than managing her own needs, desires, feelings, and shortcomings. It refers to the addiction I currently have to eating snacks at my desk while working! What started as a benign idea to keep a few snacks at my desk so I would not overeat later at lunch or dinner has cycled into an obsession where I feel panicked if I open my drawer and do not see any! As I sit at my desk, every time I see a complicated email or issue, I instinctively open my drawer. It has become a real issue and I never saw it coming. Now that I finally recognize it as getting out of hand, I can mindfully confront it. The circuitry of addiction is, however, once established, very challenging to correct. Had I not finally recognized and confronted my own, it could have manifested as 50 pounds of unhealthy extra weight over a few years, which then could have led to a heavy emotional toll.

The unfortunate truth about addictions is that they start with a fun, benign seeming impulsive action and then they grow into a beast of their own. As the circuitry begins to rewire, the brain forms a memory pathway. It recognizes a pattern. Example, Person A feels stressed about an argument at work. Person A reaches for a cigarette or sugary snack. The rush of dopamine feels good. This replaces the uncomfortable feeling previously there. Person A feels great now, although it is an illusion because no resolution to the argument at work has occurred. A circuit begins. Over time, the brain learns this behavior. The uncomfortable feeling is quickly and robotically resolved with a substance that causes a dopamine surge. The action becomes automated. The person no longer even employs a conscious decision. They feel stress, they automatically and without thought reach for the soothing item, much in the way a baby reaches for a pacifier.

The key to overcoming this is to continually stay mindful of our habits and interventions. Is it an intervention that serves us? Or can we replace it with a better one? If the sugary snack works, could standing up and taking 10 deep breaths also work? Could herbal tea work? What would lead to our longer-term goals and needs? It takes hard purposeful effort to retrain these habits that have become automated. It is not easy and requires us to plan a course of action before the trigger happens. For me, I can start by placing only vegetables or protein in my drawer, not crackers or cookies. For a drug addict, it is obviously a much more difficult path that almost always requires professional help.

Alcohol, smoking, and drugs not only rewire the brain in the ways we just discussed, but they also contribute to brain inflammation. Over years of abuse, the inflammation worsens. In addition to the rewiring of neural pathways that addictive behavior causes, chronic inflammation (caused by our diets, our substance abuse, and toxins) further diminishes the ability of the prefrontal cortex to do its job. As a result, it no longer seems like a bad idea to yell at your spouse or on the spur of the moment decide to quit your job. Because the impulse is no longer governed by judgment, the filter is gone.

Teenagers do not have fully developed prefrontal cortexes. As a result, even when they know the consequences, often they are unable to stop themselves from engaging in impulsive, risky behavior. Alcoholics have unknowingly regressed themselves to their teen years, by damaging their prefrontal cortex with brain inflammation. Just like teens, they can be charming, fun, lovable, moody, and utterly untrustworthy! Disturbingly, some studies have even shown that overuse of screen time, especially in children, prematurely thins the cortex, potentially resulting in impulsivity, lower IQ, and premature aging of the brain.

Although alcohol and smoking are big factors, brain inflammation can be caused by several sources. Excessive sugar is one.

A teenager who smokes, drinks, and loves sugar may really struggle with impulsivity and risky behavior, due to having many variables affecting their pre-frontal cortex decision making. Even if the teen does not engage in inappropriate behavior, their brain inflammation may cause them to really struggle with motivation, depression, lack of goal setting and inability to delay gratification to stick out a long difficult course (for example, college). They will likely be easily bored, emotionally over-sensitive and quick to throw in the towel when things become tough.

But you may be asking, how is any of this relevant to managing our emotions? It's two-fold.

One, if we find ourselves personally struggling with any of the above characteristics, there is hope. Reducing brain inflammation is one step toward being able to develop discipline, and that may require professional help and medications, at least for awhile, to restabilize the brain chemistry. The real rewards in life (good health, financial stability, long-term close relationships with family and friends, career advancement, emotional and spiritual growth) all come from the steady pursuit of discipline. It comes from making the daily choices of eggs instead of Fruit Loops for breakfast, tuna instead of donuts, working out instead of scrolling through Instagram for two hours, investing money instead of splurging on trends. All those choices are difficult, but they add up to long, rich rewards. Understanding that brain inflammation is a part of the cycle that both causes and is affected by our choices, helps us understand how to get on track.

Interestingly, highly processed foods like fast foods and junk foods create low energy, which in turn creates apathy. We raise kids in drive-through restaurants and then wonder why they lack motivation and drive! Unprocessed foods like fruits, vegetables and lean meats are well-absorbed by the body and contain the enzymes and micro-nutrients needed so that our food can create energy.

Understand that we are ALL easily trapped by one addictive behavior or another. We are all subject to the array of temptations all around us that become more and more accessible each day. Happiness does not come from indulgence. In fact, over self-indulgence leads to the greatest misery and self-loathing of all. Happiness comes from finding joy in the small things, the important things. It comes from fulfillment and self-discipline. It helps to self-reflect on our habits and see whether they are habits that serve us. Are they habits progressing us toward more of what we want to become? Or less? Are they habits that serve ourselves AND those around us? Or ones that only serve our ego? Or ones that cause deterioration and destruction?

What habits do you have right now that you feel are causing you to be less than who you wish to be?

_____

_____

Release any judgement or self-loathing you may feel about this. Accept that it is part of being human. Be grateful that you are mindful enough to be aware of this habit that is not serving you. How will you change it? What will you do today to start?

Even more importantly, what will you replace this habit with? What will your new reward be? What will the long-term benefits be of this replacement? Nature does not like a void. It is virtually impossible to "quit" or "take away" something successfully without replacing it with something else that the brain also will recognize as a reward. See if you can find a visual image online that represents this and print it out. Keep it somewhere that you can look at it often. Figure out the perfect replacement reward for each habit you wish to change and incorporate that. For example, if your habit is to come home and drink a beer every night, create a new habit for that same time of day. It must be a habit you are excited about. Once you replace the habit, it will take about 21 times of doing this before your brain is rewired to the new pattern and automatically reaches for the new habit over the old one.

If you find yourself repeatedly choosing to do what feels good (social media scrolls) over what serves you and your future (exercising, working on education, working on career, building relationships, improving nutrition, finances, or spiritual growth), your results will continue to disappoint you. Each time you are engaged in an activity, ask yourself if it is serving you.

This brings us to another critical message. Whether we like it or not, no matter how healthy our lifestyle is, sometimes the only way to feel better and achieve true stability is through professional help. Once our brains have chemical neurotransmitter imbalances, or trauma-based wiring, or even well hardened limiting mindset pathways, often medications and/or therapy are the only answer. I have lost count of the number of friends who, in the past few years, finally sought professional help and for the first time in decades now feel free, light, productive and creative. These are friends who all lived very healthily, made good choices, and tried hard to be their best. Despite their efforts, they still struggled with anxiety, depression, anger, instable moods, or apathy. Every single friend I have had who has started therapy and medication has transformed before my eyes. It was a wonderful thing to see.

I watched a 25-year-old who had struggled with feelings of worthlessness, violent bouts of anger and inability to complete any project transform into a kind, loving, happy, extremely productive adult. This after only 8 weeks of consistent therapy and the right stabilizing medication. The mood swings of the past decade vanished, and she became consistently content and focused.

I watched a 50-year-old who continually battled her own lack of joy and often felt guilty about it and tried to hide it, transform into radiance. She started therapy and meds and three months later said she has truly never felt better.

Many think medications are dangerous or there are too many side effects. In some cases that may be true, but science is usually the right answer to most intractable problems. Restabilizing hormones or neurotransmitter balance is a very tricky thing to do by purely alternative methods, especially since it is almost impossible to truly measure brain neurotransmitters. Medications, on the other hand, can go straight to the root of the imbalance and stabilize the situation enough so the person feels relief and can have the energy and motivation to be even more diligent with self-care.

Similarly, we can try to work out our own self-destructive thought patterns but rarely is it as effective as having a professional walk us through that journey, pointing out our patterns and mal adaptions in the moment. They can also provide homework and exercises to help us rewire our brain. They keep us accountable and provide a safe space for us to process and grow.

Knowledge is power.

Psychology Today, Austin Perlmutter, MD How Inflammation Changes Our Thinking Feb 11, 2020

Inflammation Predicts Decision-Making Characterized by Impulsivity, Present Focus and an Inability to Delay Gratification, Gassen, et al., ncbi. nlm.nih.gov

CHAPTER 11

Good Vibrations and Mindset

INSTEAD OF PUTTING OUR FOCUS ON OTHER PEOPLE AND ON situations, what if we put all our focus on raising our own vibration level. What does that mean?

Everything in the universe is energy and all energy has its own vibration level. An analogy is smell. Think about what fresh baked cinnamon rolls smell like. Now think about what rotten milk smells like. Think about what each one attracts. Fresh baked cinnamon rolls attract smiles and happiness and warmth as we flock around them with mouths drooling. Rotten milk attracts a cringe and a grimace and a quick toss as far away from us as we can get.

Your vibration level is similar. I had a saying for my daughters when they were young. "The universe is like a boomerang. Whatever you throw out there will fly back and land in your lap." ("or smack you in the face").

Your vibration level is the type of energy you are emitting. Is it angry? Resentful? Loving? Joyful? Grateful? Enthusiastic? Apathetic?

Whatever you are putting out there is likely what you will attract back, perpetuating the cycle.

Ironically, for whatever reason, when we are most annoyed with our significant other or family for petty things, it is usually because we have abandoned ourselves by not taking care of ourselves and listening to and meeting our needs. We feel uncomfortable but rather than do the work to take care of our own needs, it feels much easier to point fingers and require someone else to meet our needs. We do this unconsciously but in the process can act like real jerks.

As one example, let's say we have neglected our personal exercise for several weeks. We may begin noticing how our significant other eats unhealthy or is messy. We fixate on their flaws. We assume the anxiousness we feel inside due to our own lack of exercise is caused by our significant other's "flaws." We feel if we "fix" them, they'll make us feel better. False. The issue is usually with us, not them. No matter how perfect they become, we will feel the same unless we resolve our own issues.

Another example is if we have a stressful environment at work. We internalize the stress and when we come home, we feel triggered by what we formerly found to be minor issues, such as kids leaving clothes everywhere or not putting dishes away. Our anger and frustration at them rages, but in reality the source of our feelings are our own work issues that we need to take the time to thoughtfully resolve. Think how much emotional pain we cause to our loved ones by not taking time to go inward and find our true source of angst, before flinging it out to others.

Common sources of angst and triggers are skipping meals, not eating enough protein and healthy food, not drinking enough water, not getting enough sleep, hormonal changes, lack of exercise and not taking time to reflect and plan and be. If you find yourself commonly angered or dealing with extreme triggers, try to track your trends and self-care, related to these core physical needs.

Every being and living thing in the universe has energy and a certain vibrational frequency. Have you ever been in the presence of someone who makes you cringe? Where you feel uneasy by their mere presence? Odds are their vibrational level was far different than yours. Those who harbor great negativity, a critical voice or resentment emit a low vibration level. Those who practice gratitude and consistent self-care emit a higher vibration level.

Everything contributes to our vibration level; from the food we eat to the people we associate with to the music we listen to. Healthy food, adequate sleep, daily exercise, and mindfulness/meditation all raise our vibration level. We feel better and are thereby better equipped to care more about others.

When we choose a gratitude mindset over a victim mindset, we can thrive in any setting. Have you ever noticed how many highly accomplished people seem to be universally positive and filled with gratitude? Usually, people think they are that way because their lives are so successful and bountiful. Think again! They first made the choice to be positive and grateful, regardless of their circumstances. Success and inspiration then followed, as opportunity and the right people became attracted to their positive energy.

Having a critical voice, towards others or to ourselves, is one of the most damaging and low-level things we can do. Talk to yourself like you would your best friend. Really think about that. What if you choose your words and thoughts about yourself, with the same degree of care you show toward the words you speak to your best friend? Your brain believes what you say and what you think. How much better would you feel every day, if you became your own biggest fan?

One of the best ways to make gratitude a habit is by journaling. Throughout the day we are confronted with a litany of events, people, words, and stimuli. Our brain struggles to process it all. The aspects we do not have a logical explanation for our brain may want to ruminate on. Rumination can be extremely exhausting and often leads to no clear answers. It is most common when confronted with relationship issues. The reality is, matters of the heart are rarely resolved by the brain. Often there actually is no logical explanation or solution.

A good method to "empty" is to journal all your thoughts. This "dumps" them from your brain which frees up mental processing. Once you have emptied your thoughts, go into your heart, and determine what you feel. Is it fear? Anger? Resentment? Grief? Shame? Guilt? Worry? Once you know what the feeling is, decide how to address it. If it is grief, perhaps therapy would be appropriate. If it is fear, what actions can you take to resolve the situation, without looking toward someone else to "save" you or "fix" it for you? If it is shame or guilt, ask yourself and your higher power, if you believe in that, for forgiveness. You cannot change the past, but you do not have to carry the feelings of the past into the future. We all make mistakes; we all encounter struggles. It is how we process those and move forward that matters.

Going back to your Thing, from the end of Chapter 2. Can you use this exercise to work through your Thing?

The concept of properly processing struggles and mistakes leads us to its sister concept, that of mindset. I cannot overexpress the massive power of mindset. Mindset trumps willpower, every time. What is the difference?

I recently attended a conference where the speaker, Randy Pope, offered a tantalizing insight. He gave an analogy about teaching someone to golf. He told the student that no matter how good of a teacher he was and not matter how much the student practiced, the result would not be successful unless the student used proper grip, posture, and alignment. Similarly, he went on to say, no matter how many workshops and self-help books we consume, our full potential will never be realized unless we have an aligned and useful view of ourselves, our higher power, and our world. This relates to mindset. For if we have a poor view of ourselves, our willpower alone will soon falter for almost any difficult goal we set. Our negative self-talk quickly overpowers willpower. With the correct mindset, however, willpower becomes automatic and unflinching. Willpower helps us do hard things. Mindset helps us see hard things as easy. Let's look at some examples:

Exercising. If one sees exercise as a chore, it can be difficult to maintain the willpower necessary to be consistent. Willpower, after all, ebbs, and flows. It is not a constant. It is heavily impacted by fatigue, stress, nutrition, priorities, and several other variables.

If one, however, views exercise as an exciting and fun treat, no willpower is needed to complete the task. I learned this years ago when I made the switch from mind-numbing workouts in the gym to social runs outdoors with friends. Just like that, running went from an agonizing item on my to do list to something I really looked forward to and even craved. No more willpower needed, and I even went on to run 100-mile adventure races. I never would have dreamed I had that ability during my former years of crunching out tedious miles on a treadmill. Changing my mindset and environment was truly a game changer.

One of the secrets to hacking life is to make every important habit part of a mindset platform.

Work. Similarly, if we see work as a paycheck, it can feel like a soul – sucking aspect of our lives. This is why most people dread Monday and love Fridays. This is due to their mindset. If work is just a paycheck to you, of course it will feel like a tedium trap. What if, however, you see it as an opportunity? An opportunity to network with people, lead others, come up with creative ideas, and build your skills and abilities? What if, with this new mindset, you spent every drive to work listening to podcasts geared to helping you become better at what you do, no matter what that is? What if you mapped out some goals for work, perhaps not even goals to advance yourself, but rather goals to advance your team and the company you work for? What if you felt really truly grateful for the opportunity to work in a temperature-controlled, safe, and free atmosphere? Truly grateful for the richness and purpose work can add to your life. What if you saw every frustration at work as an interesting challenge to be navigated? A giant chess game? Suddenly work becomes fun. Again, no willpower needed.

Willpower to do hard things requires tremendous energy. When we see everything in our lives as a chore, a difficulty or a hardship, we quickly become exhausted due to all the willpower we are having to expend to do the basic tasks of life. This is quickly reversed when we change our mindset and make hard things fun and desirable to do.

Sex. This may seem like it does not need to go on this list, but you would be surprised. Because men and women are wired differently, I know a lot of amazing women who find sex with their partners to be a tiring and unfulfilling chore. They feel guilt and frustration for feeling this way, yet the feeling is real. It's a very real struggle. The fact is men and women are wired differently. Sex is often a craving for men while for women it can ebb and flow based on a plethora of variables. The dichotomy occurs when women feel guilted into having sex anytime the man wants it, even if she isn't feeling it. Over time this breeds frustration and resentment, requiring the woman to muster yet even more willpower each time she consents to intimacy in the face of lack of desire. This is one of the most common, yet unspoken challenges in marriages, and has been since the beginning of time. And yet, what if we, as women could rework the mindset we have around sex? Our whole lives we have been taught to use sex to achieve the right partner, the lifestyle, the children. We are biologically wired to do so. Whereas men see sex as simply an enjoyable past time and one that connects the two people. This is a reason why, for men, any time is the right time, and, for women, a narrow window is the right time, one where all the chores are done, the kids are settled, the environment is romantic, and the man is meeting all their emotional needs.

What if women could see sex, on its own without an agenda, as something very good? Sex has been proven to have a ton of health and emotional benefits. It is good for the skin, the organs, vitality, and the mood. It is anti-aging. It burns calories. It balances neurotransmitters. It relaxes the mind and body. What if everyone could go into sex, every time, thinking of it as something that benefits us and as a way to bring pleasure to a partner? What if the mindset could be that sex is always good, within the confines of a safe and committed relationship? What if we could release the "requirements" we have around it and just enjoy it? Do we view a massage as a chore? Of course not. Are we ever too tired to have a massage? Of course not. Why? Because we go into it with the mindset that it feels good and benefits us. Mindset changes everything.

Parenting. This is a big one! It is easy to be overwhelmed by the neediness of little ones or the entitledness of teens. It is easy to feel exhausted, taken advantage of, worried. In this state, we become reactive. Being reactive to either of these age groups can cause irreparable harm, creating distance and even trauma. No good parent wants to do that, yet the willpower required to be consistently patient, firm, kind and loving can truly become grueling. What if we changed our mindset? Our feelings arise from our mindset that we are responsible for these mini versions of ourselves. That they are a reflection of us. But what if we changed that? What if we adopted the mindset that these are independent humans, who the universe graciously allowed into our lives for us to mentor and to bring us happiness? What if we adopted the mindset that we absolutely cannot, no matter what we do, control every aspect of their lives nor who they are nor how they reflect on us. Rather we can gently try and then simply observe. We can adopt the mindset that nothing matters more than the relationship we build with them, and the safe space we create for them within which to grow and develop. With that mindset, focused on observing their changes and building an ever-evolving relationship with them, the process becomes easy. We become curious and interested in their behavior changes. We adapt and evolve with them. We feel true gratitude and love. We relax. They relax. Everything becomes easier.

Look at every area of your life where you are having to employ great willpower and see how you can reconstruct the situation to require little or none. Think of areas where you need no willpower to get yourself to do it. Eating chocolate. Getting a massage. Watching Netflix. Why are these easy and fun? Find ways to make other areas in your life easy and fun.

I did this exercise while writing this book. There were times when I procrastinated and struggled to make myself sit down and write. So, I created a happy space wherein I could do it. I would play a funny Netflix show in the background, light a candle, drink a yummy beverage (maybe wine!) or play my favorite music (very loudly). It became an experience I looked forward to, as opposed to "work."

Give yourself grace. Change is hard. Our biologically wired instincts are to maintain the status quo and "stay safe" by not changing. One reason is because new habits require new brain wiring which requires energy. Our bodies and brains want us to minimize energy, so that we can use what we have to survive any upcoming threat. This is useful for survival yet counterproductive for growth or thriving. As a result, some studies show it takes 21 days to develop a new habit. Basically, with each new habit, you must literally re-program a naturally resistant brain.

I always find this so funny to see in practice. I remember when my teenage daughter first obtained contact lens. Her vision was only mildly near-sighted, so she was able to function without them. At the same time, for weeks after we bought her daily lens, we would be out and about and she would complain "I can't read that sign or that menu on the wall, etc." I would look at her surprisedly and say, "Do you have your contacts in?" She would giggle and look down and say "No." I would say, "Interesting, do you find it surprising you can't read far away things?" We would both laugh about it but it truly took weeks before she was able to develop the habit to incorporate something as simple as wearing her contact lens...even though she was aware how helpful they were to her. She had headaches in school from squinting and STILL struggled to develop the habit. This is normal for most of us and something we absolutely should not beat ourselves up for!

Instead, we can choose to acknowledge it, laugh it off, and implement a hack to help, even if it is as simple as a Post It note on the bathroom mirror that says, "Put contacts in!"

If a change like this was so hard for my daughter, imagine how hard it is for an alcoholic to build the habit of going to AA, or stopping drinking. Or for a person to start a new exercise routine. It is legitimately and universally hard. Having the right tips and tricks (and grace and humor for yourself) are keys.

CHAPTER 12

The Mirror (Facing Short Term Pain Erases Long Term Suffering)

DURING LIFE, WE WILL EXPERIENCE PAIN. WE WILL HAVE TO, AT times, experience grieving. What we do not have to do is choose long term suffering.

For whatever reason, humans learn the most through pain. We prefer the status quo unless forced to change. Hitting rock bottom or experiencing great grief or pain is often the most effective path toward true growth. It's unfortunate, but true.

When you are in the depths of pain or grief, you can choose to be a victim and suffer indefinitely or you can choose to surrender to the pain, feel the pain and break open into something better. You can choose to use the pain to expand your consciousness, your perspective, and your capacity for empathy.

Sometimes we attract whatever unresolved trauma resides inside us. For example, if, as a child you experienced instances where you felt abandoned, you may still carry that trauma with you. As a child you likely lacked the tools to process and release it. Even if you had the best parents, they may have been unaware you felt this trauma, or they may have themselves lacked the tools to help you process it. Our outside world is often a mirror of our inner world. This means that the unresolved trauma in your belly from childhood events is a magnet to attracting similar hurtful situations as an adult. I believe we are often required to face and acknowledge our unresolved traumas in order to release them. Until we do, the universe will continue to place us in those same situations, repeatedly.... until we can forgive and love.

Animals handle trauma very simplistically and well. Picture a herd of deer grazing. A mountain lion begins stalking them. It begins chasing a young deer. The deer, if it escapes, is terrified and traumatized. Instinctively it shakes uncontrollably. This helps release fear and trauma from its body. It then runs back to the herd where the mother deer licks it, nuzzles it and nudges it back to grazing. The other deer supportively gather around it. Trauma resolved.

The deer does not have intellect or ego to get in the way. It does not tell itself wild stories that the trauma was its own fault or that it was not worthy or that it is flawed. It does not spend the next 20 years ruminating on the experience and blaming the mountain lion. It does not stop grazing and go hide in a cave. It simply accepts that a mountain lion traumatized it, due to no fault of its own, and then it processes that trauma and goes on about the day.

We humans are far more complex. Again, due to no fault of our own. Our brains want to rationalize and analyze everything. Why did the mountain lion choose to attack me? Is there something wrong with me? Is the mountain lion evil? Am I unlovable? Why didn't the whole herd protect me? Am I not worthy? Do they not care about me? Am I not enough?

Because we are more complex, we need more help processing our trauma. Yet we resist the help. The path of least resistance is to stay locked up in our heads, analyzing and blaming. Opening to someone and sharing how very scared we felt is hard. What if they reject or judge or blame us more? For this reason, it is critically important that we create safe spaces where those we care about can share anything with us. Safe spaces where they can tell exactly how they felt and we can empathize, share their pain, hug them tight, nuzzle them and nudge them to move forward with their life. It is also very important to encourage our loved ones to go to counseling and to take medications if needed. Most people are initially resistant to this idea, but it truly does help.

If we refuse to use tools to successfully process our trauma, it floats around inside us like a grenade with the top barely hanging on. While it's floating around in there, our bodies are desperately trying to alert us to do something about it. We are likely very busy trying to ignore or compartmentalize that anxious feeling. Usually if we do notice it, we will quickly whisk away the pesky feeling with drinking, overeating, smoking, overworking, over-shopping, being overly- critical or any number of other "overs." Our bodies, though, will not take no for an answer. They continue to nudge, whether with knots of anxiety or headaches or backaches or fatigue.

What are the stories we tell ourselves? Have you ever noticed that some people are happy and pleasant most of the time and others are disgruntled and sarcastic most of the time? Ironically, the external circumstances do not seem to be variable. Many of the happiest, most gratitude filled people are also the ones who have undergone the most trauma and difficulties.

A classic example is of the concentration camp survivor Joseph Alexander. During his experience he suffered food deprivation, isolation, torture and even being urinated on. Most of the other victims died. He did not. How did he survive? He says he never lost faith and he never carried a grudge. He says it doesn't help anything; it just makes you sick.

Here's an example in physical terms: Have you ever had a rock in your shoe? The pesky thing moves around as you walk so that sometimes you don't feel at all and then sometimes it reminds you with a sharp stab. Sometimes it is purely excruciating. Then it moves again, and you forget about it. In the back of your mind though, it's there. It is distracting and disconcerting. It keeps you from taking off into a full sprint. It holds you back.

It is the exact same way with emotional baggage. Think about Marilyn Monroe. She most likely had borderline personality disorder (BPD), a highly frustrating condition that is often thought to develop as a survival response to childhood trauma, real or perceived. In many ways, and on the surface, she was everything one would want to be. Powerful, beautiful, charming, magnetic, successful. On the inside, she was a swirling storm of conflicting thoughts, toxic feelings, and insecurities. She had doctors and medications but at the time they did not have the level of understanding and ability to treat conditions like BPD using techniques we have now, like Dialectical Behavior Therapy. Additionally, borderlines are notoriously stubborn about resisting treatment. They have subconsciously developed these emotional storms to deal with their pain and they are not able to imagine anything else. They are trapped in their own storm. The rock is in their shoe creating a festering wound and they refuse to let anyone help them take the shoe off because they are so terrified of seeing their naked foot. Frightened of facing their own trauma and processing it.

How do we help someone who is trapped in this way? We provide them with a safe space and firm boundaries. We reassure without enabling. We remind without nagging. We don't back down. We keep helping them see the vision of what life could be like with no rock in their shoe and no insecurities paralyzing their joy. We help them look in the mirror and see their potential and uniqueness the way we see it.

One of the hardest, yet most rewarding ways to use this theory is in conflict. In conflict, we experience a lot of very uncomfortable feelings. Fear, anger, contempt, resentment, grief. The path of least resistance is to run. To leave the situation. Or to numb by finding an escape like food, sex, alcohol, entertainment, or excess work. A third common path of least resistance is to act out as a means of control. How many times have you experienced a significant other doing this? Acting out as a means of control can look like pouting, shutting down, saying "you always do this" or becoming violent. These tactics are used because the person has not yet learned how to face the discomfort and have the bravery to internally process it and maturely communicate about it.

Acting out as a means of control feels like a resolution of short-term pain but it leads to years of suffering for both parties. Acting out gives the other person no chance to be better. When the first person faces their own uncomfortable feelings and processes them, and then communicates about them to the other person, there is an opportunity for the other person to change and for the whole relationship to grow and mature.

Acting out resolves nothing. It creates a standoff. Facing, processing, and communicating about feelings is truly fighting for a relationship. It is for this reason we developed the "Don't Shout It Out, Write It Out" relationship rescue notepads to help couples do exactly this.

I often hear people say they "fought for their relationship." When questioned further, you find out they cried nightly, moved out, or threatened killing themselves. That is not fighting for a relationship.

That is fighting to avoid your own personal growth. It is being afraid to look in the mirror and face yourself. It is acting out. It's immaturity.

I say that without judgment. Almost all of us have experienced pain from conflict that felt unbearable. Facing it fully in the short term is hard and it is a learned skill. We, unlike animals, are not inherently born knowing how to handle trauma.

If we want to be happy, and be able to contribute to others' happiness, we have to learn how.

As you experience each of life's challenges, look in the mirror and ask yourself the following questions:

What is the trigger?

What do you feel in your body in response to the trigger?

What is the behavior instinct reaction you experience? Run? Fight? Act out? Be violent?

What is the behavior reaction that your highest self would employ? Your most mature self?

What is your desired goal or outcome for this scenario?

What is it you seek to feel?

How else can you get to that feeling, perhaps without relying on the other person?

What mindset would best serve you in this situation?

What story would best serve you in this situation?

CHAPTER 13

Using Empathy to Be a Really Good Human

ONCE YOU HAVE LEARNED TO MANAGE YOUR EMOTIONS AND REIN in your ego, you are ready to level up to empathy. The difference between ego and empathy is selfless love. Someone once told me when I was young that they thought I was incapable of love. That I was so goal-driven and task-oriented, that the ability to love simply wasn't on my radar. That stung. I spent a good bit of time reflecting on that statement. I came to the realization that, in truth, I really did not have a solid definition in my head of what love even was. After much reflection I finally came to this conclusion:

Love is taking patient time to listen and truly know someone, and then do what it takes to meet their needs. To put forth the curious effort to know them like no one else can, and because of that, be able to respond to them like no one else can.

This is my personal definition. Take time to develop your own. And then live it. Live it toward yourself and toward those closest to you.

One of the hardest yet most important things you'll ever do for someone you love is to try to find the best way to help them when they are suffering from emotional overload. It may be a teenager suffering from anxiety and depression, a spouse suffering from low self-esteem, a parent suffering from loss or grief or even someone who is in a manic mode and is impulsive and risk-taking.

How do you help, from a platform of pure empathy and selfless love?

First, remember that unacknowledged feelings never go away. They escalate. They pop out in unintended ways. Feelings that are acknowledged, on the other hand, gently float away because they have served their purpose, which is to remind us of our core traits and to realign us on our authentic path.

When you find that someone is sad, anxious, angry, or fearful, it is your role as an empathetic human to see if you can facilitate them into acknowledging their feelings. It is important to avoid being triggered because that typically means you have inserted your own feelings into their situation. Become curious, even intrigued by what they are experiencing. Leave all judgment at the door. Use this as an opportunity to get to know this person better, which in turn helps them get to know themselves better. Help them realize how their perceived weaknesses or struggles are often actually their greatest gifts.

Real life examples:

A young adult you are close to tells you she feels unsupported, like she always had to be the adult growing up because her parents were so chaotic. Now, as a young adult, she has lingering feelings of being on an island, without help, alone.

To explore this with her, *first validate*: "I know that had to have been so hard and painful. You should not have had to experience that and yet I am so incredibly proud of who you've become because of the way you cope with it. I suspect that's why you study so hard and have such a strong, focused work ethic. That is going to make you such a powerful resourceful adult who will be able to help so many people."

Next, *explore deeper* with them by asking questions: "When you feel that way, what does it feel like inside? What is the physical sensation? Is it emptiness? Knots? Tension? Where is it in your body? What is the very first time in your life you ever felt that? Close your eyes and try to feel the feeling and take deep breaths. Really experience it."

Next, *empower*: "When you feel that feeling, know that, because you are no longer a child, you can soothe that feeling yourself now. You have that power. You are incredibly competent at taking care of yourself. And you also have me. What do you need from me to help ease that feeling?"

In other words, rarely is it helpful to try to give solutions or fix the issue. That takes away the other person's power. Rather, empower her to verbalize the sensation, the issue, and the answers. She has the answers inside. She just needs someone to help her sit in the feeling and connect with it, to see what her inner self is trying to tell her.

Always speak strong positive words, even about uncomfortable feelings like sadness, anxiousness, or anger. The feelings are not a negative thing on their own. They are part of her person. In our example, this person may find that often when she is anxious, it is because she is so conscientious and wants to do a good job. That is a great thing. That kind of anxiety deserves praise rather than talking her out of feeling it.

Example: "I'm really worried about my test. The other kids are smarter than me."

Your response: "Of course you're anxious about your test. That's because you are so conscientious and hardworking and motivated. That's awesome. What can I do to help you prepare?"

Example: "I am sad because there is so much chaos when I'm at my parent's house."

Your response: "Of course you're sad. That's because you have a huge heart, and you care. Do you feel like you want your parent to be happy, but you don't know how to help them? That's tough. Do you think there's anything you can do to help them? Do you think they have to help themselves? What do you think your parent could do to help themselves? What physical sensations do you feel in your body in that setting, when the drama is happening? Close your eyes and breathe deep and try to recreate that. Now relax and think it through … is there anything in your power you can do to change that situation? What?"

The goal is never to fix the other person's problem.

It is to empower them to sit in their feelings until they arrive at resolution of the feeling. Only the person experiencing the feeling can resolve the feeling. You cannot do it for them. You are only the facilitator.

Example: Teenager says: "I feel like my friends are so immature. I always feel like I am the one telling them not to drink and drive and to think before they act. It's hard on me."

Your response: "Good. We call that leadership. I love that it's obviously hardwired into you. Never apologize for that. The world needs more of you."

If you tell someone like this they need to "chill out" and "relax," you are confusing their identity. This is their gift, and who they are hardwired to be. Let it be.

Again, one of the hardest parts of this is managing our own triggers in the process. It is easy to become frustrated with the other person or judge their mood or thoughts.

Case Study: A friend told me a story the other day about her teenage daughter. The mom is an accomplished professional and the daughter is smart, beautiful, and athletic. The daughter has been a straight-A student her whole life and, of course, her parents aspire for her to have an impressive career. Lately, when the mom asks the daughter about her career aspirations, the daughter has been making comments like, "I think I want to be a stripper, they make like $700 a night," or "I just want to marry someone wealthy and take his money." The mom is instantly heartbroken, terrified, and angry. She inserts her own feelings and reacts. "What?? After all we have given you? How can you think that way? That is awful and ridiculous." The situation escalates.

What should happen is a safe conversation instead. The mom could have calmly responded, "Interesting, what appeals to you about that?" "Do you feel stressed or overwhelmed about career possibilities?" "Are you worried college will be hard?" This encourages the daughter to share her thoughts, even the crazy ones, and know she will be heard. This is empathy. This is setting aside our own agenda and fears to truly hear the other person out. This lets the other person process and is a far more effective way to help them make solid decisions.

Let's talk about therapy for a minute. No one ever WANTS to go to therapy. In fact, most people are extremely resistant to it. Why is that? The way we think, believe and act is a part of who we are, a part of our identity. The act of admitting we should seek therapy forces us to adopt the realization that our identity needs help. Subconsciously we revolt at the thought of someone telling us to think differently. It is a very primitive and understandable reaction. Our thought processes have developed over the decades of our life, often for our very survival.

The thought of releasing our safety nets of defensiveness, sarcasm, criticism, bullying, finger-pointing, self-loathing, self—harm, fear, anger, resentment, arrogance, or narcissism is, well, terrifying. We developed all that for a reason, right? Right. All those traits were developed because of modeling what we saw or as a survival mechanism to handle frightening situations. It got us through. It is primitive. And now it is time to level up. Now it is time to evolve into a wise, mature, thoughtful human who cares about others, is brave enough to face our own feelings and who communicates effectively.

As babies we do not want to learn to eat our peas or to be alone or to sleep. We fight it all. We kick, we cry, we yell, and we stomp our feet through all the things we must learn. Hopefully we have loving parents who require us to learn them anyway. Just because you are an adult does not mean that the journey is over. It has just begun. With the right therapy and coaching, you can evolve into someone who feels everything powerfully, who loves profoundly and who changes the world by words and actions. With no therapy or coaching, you are likely to stay stuck at a single digit emotional age.

Why? There is no possible way to get there on your own. Our own brains are limited in our ability to see our strengths and our shortcomings. We need the insight of others. Without purposeful outside help, our brain will keep us stuck in the safe zone, will keep looping the same thoughts, will keep activating the same patterns.

This is why you, we, all of us need therapy, coaches, mentors, and accountability groups if we want to grow. Therapy forces us to stop and ask "why" we think what we think, feel what we feel and do what we do. Often, within that process, we learn another way that may be more useful to us. This process is massively instrumental in transforming from a person who is reactive to a person who is powerfully impactful.

What about psychiatric medications? Science is a tool, and a very useful one. Over the centuries we have massively increased life span, eradicated diseases, and increased quality of life. If everyone ate perfectly, exercised regularly and generally took ideal care of themselves, our health as a society would be infinitely better and yet, we would still need science. Even in ancient Egypt, long before environmental carcinogens and cigarettes, scientists were removing brain tumors. We would still have to fix broken bones and numerous other interventions. We are humans and we are physical. We need help. Our brain is no different than our body. In the same way that sometimes medical interventions are needed for our body, sometimes they are needed for our brain. Our brain is essentially a circuit board. It has its own form of wires and computer chips and pathways. Sometimes, for whatever reason, something isn't firing right. The number of possibilities is infinite. A shortage of neurotransmitters like serotonin or dopamine, an imbalance of hormones like testosterone or estrogen, a brain lesion or tumor or blocked circuitry. A traumatic mental or physical injury. A lack of minerals and fatty acids. There are innumerable reasons why sometimes the only fix and the right fix is to take medications, even if for a limited period. Postpartum depression is a great example. The extreme toll pregnancy can take on a woman's mineral stores and hormones can send the brain into a tailwind. Willpower to "be happy" is not the answer. Restoring an optimum chemical balance, by the right medications when necessary, may be the only way.

Never, ever let someone shame or stigmatize you for taking appropriately prescribed medications, as an adjunct to taking care of yourself. Even more important, do not shame or stigmatize yourself. Prescribed medications are one more tool in your self-care toolbox.

Our jails are a poignant example of this. There is a common term in the jail community called recidivism. Recidivism means the inmates keep cycling in and out of jail, repeatedly. A large reason for this is untreated mental health conditions. Many inmates have mental health conditions that may have started as simply teenage anxiety or depression. If they did not have the right help to process these normal feelings, they may have begun to self-medicate with alcohol or drugs. Over time the brain becomes accustomed to, and re-wires itself, in the presence of the alcohol or drugs. The brain becomes completely altered. It then finds that it needs more and more of the alcohol or drugs to achieve the same desired numbing effect. Over time, the person's actions become solidly aligned with the pursuit of the alcohol or drugs to the exclusion of all else, including family, education, or employment. By the time they enter jail, their brains have often become so reconstructed that to get them back to place of "normal" they need medications. While in jail, they often get sober, get on medications, and become remarkably pleasant. They then leave the jail and stop taking their meds either because they feel fine and think they no longer need them or because they lack the financial resources to obtain them. They then begin to re-experience their mental health condition, re-seek drugs and alcohol to numb the feelings and the cycle resumes.

Medications are, for many, critical to help the brain find calm, in the same way pacemakers are critical for those whose heart beats erratically.

One of the best things that ever happened to me was meeting the founders of KultureCity, a non-profit devoted to sensory inclusion for those with autism and sensory challenges. I met one of the founders on a group run and I will never forget the first thing I learned from her. To meet people where they are. She educated me on the importance of focusing more on teaching the world how to appreciate, understand and include those who were neuro diverse, rather than focusing on only trying to "cure" this complex condition. It was one of the greatest lessons I have ever learned, and it applies to so many other situations. Rather than trying to fix or force others to be like us, when we employ empathy, we learn how to see others in all their perfection, exactly as they are. We then have open eyes and ears that can learn from them. It is in that place that the possibilities become infinite.

CHAPTER 14

Yes, Teens are Lovable and Trustable (Are You?)

IS ANY AGE DEMOGRAPHIC MORE MISUNDERSTOOD AND MIS-managed than teens? We have all been teens and yet they continue to be the most stressful years, both from the standpoint of the teens themselves and the groups trying to manage them (parents, coaches, employers, educators). Even though most of us were frustrated by our parents' tactics when we were teens, we find ourselves as parents reverting to the same fear-based philosophies. When do we, as a society, commit to getting better at raising teens? Although most of us have learned that teen brains do not develop until mid-twenties, that they naturally are wired to seek independence from us, and that their brains are impulsive, we still find ourselves angry when they push back. We confront them and demand conformity, demand that they fall into line and be subservient like when they were younger. Maybe some of the problem is with us, not them.

What if we put ourselves into their shoes for a moment? What if we thought back to our own teen years and remembered the complexity of hormones, emotions, triggers and drives we felt? What if we worked WITH them instead of against them? Not as their "friends" but as their coaches, guides, and mentors. What if instead of trying to force them to be 40-year-old responsible counterparts of ourselves, we recognized that they are not that and are not going to be that while in their teens? What if we asked more questions and offered fewer lectures? What if we told them about the great things that will happen if they do x, y and z rather than constantly scare them with statements like, "If you don't get good grades you won't get into college or get a good job"? What an uninspiring statement yet how many of us have said it? We could rephrase it by saying, "you have really good (judgment/work ethic/ instincts/ personality). As you keep developing that you are going to have more and more opportunities to choose from. I'm excited to see where that leads for you. What are you most interested in now?"

When one of my daughters was a teen, I remember being worried about every change I saw. She went through a period of being withdrawn and staying in her room more and I went through extreme worry. I peppered her with questions which drove her crazy and caused her to stay in her room even more. I finally recognized that nothing was "wrong." She simply was getting older. She no longer wanted to be at my shoulder as much and that was normal. In her room she was usually on video chat talking to her friends, or playing with makeup or any number of things that she began to prefer rather than spending time with me. I was the one with the problem adjusting to this natural evolution of her growth. I was the one over-analyzing and worrying about it. She was simply developing. I finally stopped all the incessant "are you okay" questions and simply gave her information. "I'm here if you need me. Dinner will be ready at 7. Let me know if you'd like me to help with your homework." It took a few weeks, but she began to open up and, of her own accord, spend more time with me. She did this because she no longer felt pressured.

We often put unreasonable expectations and pressure on teens when we would be better served by inspiring them. Do we need to hold them accountable? Certainly. Can we do it in a respectful, thoughtful way? Yes. Keep this basic humane premise in mind: Innocent until proven guilty. Often, as parents, we operate under a "guilty until proven innocent" fear-driven mindset, which doesn't exactly inspire our children to trust or respect us. How many times have you assumed facts that were not true, blowing up at your child and later finding out you were exaggerating the situation in your own mind? Parents do this all the time. We recently had a teen spend the night at our house. At one point during the night, the teen's phone died. She left it on a charger while the kids took the golf cart up to our neighborhood clubhouse. Within an hour her parents were texting me in a panic. I was on a call and could not respond right away. Within 30 minutes they were at our house, picking her up and yelling at her for not answering her phone. Unbelievable. This is an incredibly mature, hardworking, straight A student. To have so little trust and to assume the worst so quickly is a sure way to destroy your relationship with your child.

One study found that the simple act of asking a student whether they were planning to go to college significantly increased their odds of going to college. Asking people who they are going to vote for significantly increases their odds of voting. Perhaps asking more and demanding less is the way we help our teens find their path. Why would we choose to make aggressive demands to an individual whose brain we know is biologically more wired toward pushing back and seeking independence now than at any other point in their lives? Forcing teens into compliance is fraught with problems. Empowering them to do the right thing and the best thing is the way to winning their hearts.

Teens may act like they no longer need us, but they do. They crave a safe, reassuring place to decompress from all the stressors and incredible peer pressure they face. They want to know we respect them and believe in them. They want our life advice but in small, very small, doses, where we talk with them, not at them. They need a safe place to share what they are comfortable with and know they will be listened to, not judged.

But how do we do that when everything in us is in heightened alert because of the dangers they are starting to explore? Our parental brains are on fire with worst cases scenarios of teen pregnancy, STDs, alcohol overdose, experimental drugs that cause lifelong brain chemistry changes and more. We are constantly afraid they'll make grades too low to get into college or get arrested for being with the wrong crowd or run over someone while driving. It's a lot. It's a lot for us and a lot for them. So how about if everyone takes a deep breath and agrees to work on this together instead of in an adversarial way? If we constantly spill all our fears on them, they will not see us as a safe place. Imagine if every time you went to your boss with a concern or idea, he did a brain dump on you about how if you don't do your job perfectly, he may lose customers and not have revenue and not be able to pay you and go out of business? How overwhelming would that be? What a downer. Would you want to have a connection with that employer? Would you feel safe with them? Would you go to them for inspiration and ideas? Probably not. You would likely retreat and, over time, tell them less and less. Eventually you would find a different job.

As much as we want our teens to control themselves, we need to control ourselves even more. We need to manage our own fear. We need to relinquish control over every outcome. We need to be prepared for the reality that they will make mistakes, probably many of them. We need to give them the space and security to let us help them help themselves.

Keep this in mind. Teens are fighting for the moment. You're fighting for their future. The two are not going to align, and you are not going to "win" by being overbearing or controlling. You win by listening, asking why, helping them come to the right conclusions themselves and by facilitating their thought process through questions.

I was recently on the plane with a friend. She was talking about her 13-year-old daughter and how frustrated she was that her daughter was always in her room or on her phone. The mom admitted she was alternating between getting angry at her daughter and obsessively worrying that something was wrong with her. I smiled. Because this story is so incredibly common. The mom is single, with no other children in the household. I said, "How does it make you feel when you are alone in the house, and she is upstairs in her room?" The mom looked at me thoughtfully. "I feel so lonely," she said. I smiled. Then it hit her. The problem was not that her daughter was maturing into a normal teenager, developing independence. There was nothing wrong with her daughter at all. The problem was that mom had not moved on with her life to adapt to her daughter's changing dependence on her. I smiled and said, "Maybe it's time for some new hobbies and friends for Mom." She started to smile and cry at the same time and said, "I think I just had an a-ha moment and I'm so grateful I now know how to quit taking this out on my daughter." The reality is, once Mom starts adapting and changing, daughter will come back around. Mom just needs to step back and give her a little space to grow. Mom needs to let daughter know she is there for her, all the time, but she will no longer be helicoptering and guilt-tripping her daughter into spending every waking moment with her.

A few weeks later I ran into this same mom in a work restroom. She stopped and looked at me with the most heartfelt gaze and said, "You gave me the best advice I have ever had. She comes to me now. We have the best talks. Thank you from the bottom of my heart."

Trust me, this advice is easier to give than to do. I spent a solid year working on my relationship with one of my daughters during her early teens to learn to restrain my reactions, my fears, and my demands. Prior to the purposeful work on myself, and following my divorce, she had become avoidant, cold, and minimally affectionate. She rarely responded to texts from me and spent most of her time at home in her room. She rarely even referred to me as Mom, preferring instead to say "hey." A year later we laugh and talk together every day. She responds to me quickly. We have fun nicknames for each other. Our relationship is easy and relaxed. She communicates with me before she is asked. She opens up about her friendships and relationships. She matured but I also changed how I was interacting with her. I pulled back and created a safe, non-reactive space. This does not mean I still do not set every parental boundary needed. I do, but I try to do so in a non-reactive, non-fearful, calm way. When I set boundaries she does not like now, we are able to laugh about how much she does not like them. She accepts the boundaries and jokes about them, even with her friends. Yet she respects them because she respects my role. Because of our heightened communication, she now understands those boundaries come from a reasonable place of love, not a place of unreasonable fear-based control.

I focus now much more on helping her build herself, rather than the "what-ifs" of the potential dangers. We talk about the dangers of sex, drugs, alcohol, and distracted driving, yes, but we spend far more time talking about how the world could solve social problems, what careers are most fulfilling, what her skills and talents are and how to develop into her best.

Shout out here to Dr. RJ Jackson, an orthodontist and psychologist turned teen life coach. His online classes are a great resource to helping teens develop confidence and motivation, which are your two greatest allies for keeping them from resorting to substance abuse or reckless behaviors.

Every teen I ever knew growing up, including myself, faced episodes of anxiety and sadness and insecurity and fear. That is simply part of life. I do not know anyone who hasn't experienced these things. They are normal human emotions. We just didn't label it or dwell on it back then. We had no choice, and our parents gave us no choice, other than to face it and fight through it and go be productive anyway. Now teens have an abundance of choices. Avoid life and play on their phones all day. Live at home till they're thirty. Wallow in their fears and self-created limitations, secondary to their labels.

We've given them lives filled with every creature comfort imaginable and then we wonder why they lack drive. Drive is borne from need. If we supply every need, they will have no drive.

As with other areas of your life, your mindset is the determining indicator of your reactions. Is your goal to build a strong relationship with your teen and help them reach their full potential? Or is to control them and show them who is boss? Is it to meet your own needs through them or to help them develop? Ask yourself these questions before you react and it will start to become easier to react from a place that is truly focused on them, and not on your own fears and worries.

There are thousands of stories of parents overreacting and failing to hear the full truth of the situation teens go through. Listen. Don't judge. Ask thoughtful questions in a calm way, not as interrogation. Too many parents are hyper focused on proving their child did something wrong. This isn't the goal. The goal is to support and inspire. It is to provide fair progressive discipline in a calm manner after ALL the facts are investigated, not while you are at the height of your emotions. Avoid jumping to conclusions fueled by your own hyperactive brain. They deserve a fair trial, and they need you to be a coach as much as a parent. Remember, judgment is almost always borne of ignorance, and should almost always be replaced with curiosity and empathy.

Ask yourself if you search as often for the times they make good decisions as the times they make poor decisions? Why are we so committed to being Sherlock Holmes and tracking down their every poor choice?! Have you ever asked your teen, "What is the last good decision you made? Was it hard? How did it make you feel?" Trust me, they make good decisions far more often than you think and they are not going to tell you unless you ask. They assume you only care when they make mistakes unless you purposefully show them otherwise. Give them opportunities often to tell you about their virtues. If you open that door, they will show up more often than you would think to proudly share with you.

Most importantly, thank them. Thank them early and often, even before they do the good thing. "Thank you for often being so responsible and thinking things through. It makes me proud that you do that. Thank you for being so kind. I'm so grateful you have common sense and usually make such good choices." Saying these words rather than finding their flaws will train them to be the kind of individual you want them to be. Words are powerful. Give them words to live up to not to shrink away from.

CHAPTER 15

Attachment Theory

ONE OF THE MOST USEFUL TOOLS YOU CAN HAVE TO FULLY understand and navigate your own sometimes muddled reactions is a grasp on your attachment style. Learning about this completely changed my thought processes, my reactions, and my relationships.

Around 50 percent of us have a secure attachment style, developed in early childhood. Around 25 percent of us who are not so fortunate, have a dismissive avoidant style. Another 25 percent who are not so fortunate have an anxious needy style. Often, for a variety of reasons, a dismissive avoidant person will be highly attracted to an anxious needy person. This can result in a rather messy and drama-filled entanglement that is one part addicting and two parts toxic.

An excellent book on this is called *Attached* by Amir Levine, MD, and Rachel S.F. Heller, MA. I highly recommend either reading this book or googling attachment theory quizzes to see where you fall on the scale.

If you might be a dismissive avoidant, someone who finds more comfort in work and activities than in intimacy, know that subconsciously "distancing" yourself from an anxious needy partner can have disastrous consequences. Simple reassurance and validation, which can be extremely hard for a dismissive avoidant to do, is often all it takes to calm the drama and stabilize the other person. Instead, the temptation for a typical self-contained dismissive avoidant, is to see the anxious needy person's behaviors as weak and repulsive and attempt to shut them down.

The truth is, the dismissive avoidant person has many of the same needs and feelings as the anxious person does, it's just that their needs are effectively repressed due to their childhood experiences. Only when the anxious needy person gives up and pulls away will the dismissive avoidant's subconscious repression deactivate and true feelings surface. It is then that the avoidant will feel intense hurt and betrayal and try to win them back.

Here's a little tongue in cheek example: Being a dismissive avoidant person with an anxious needy partner is like having a new puppy. At first, the new puppy is so cute. As it gets a little older, the puppy is so enraptured by you that everywhere you walk, it is tangled up in your legs, licking and biting at your feet, not letting you take a single step. You still adore this puppy, but honestly sometimes you want to lock it in a room, so you can, for once, freely walk from the bedroom to the kitchen without being bothered. But you feel like a terrible person for even thinking about temporarily locking away this sweet puppy, especially one who loves you so! So, you grit your teeth and bear the incessant licking, biting and tangled up slow walking ... until you finally can't take it anymore and you find a puppy sitter to come stay with it so you'll have some peace. Then you get jealous because the puppy seems to like the new sitter more than you, so you want to send the puppy-sitter away. The cycle repeats, again and again. The pairing of an avoidant with an anxious attachment style often lasts a long time, although it is full of frustration and anxiety for both partners.

What the dismissive avoidant person needs is a secure three-year-old pit bull, not a sweet puppy. Strong and gentle, confident enough to assert his or her needs, loyal and yet able to give space to the avoidant. What the anxious person needs is also a secure person. A patient, reassuring secure who finds the anxious person endearing and who is willing to drop everything and reassure the anxious person on demand, as needed, until the anxious person matures from a puppy to a confident older dog. Neither person is wrong. Both simply need secure persons in their life to stabilize their extreme viewpoint on relationships. They can try to be that for each other, but odds are this will be a very uphill battle without significant professional help.

The avoidant will struggle to tolerate the intimacy that comes with working through these issues in a collaborative, not confrontational, way. The anxious will struggle with having enough grit to do the hard work and face the discomfort. The avoidant seeks to run away. The anxious person seeks instant gratification and relief from the anxiety. With professional help and patience, the couple can grow together, provided they both truly want to put forth the effort.

I recently saw a quote from Demi Moore. She said, "Bruce insisted that he thought everything about me was beautiful: he wrapped my fear and anxiety in his love. But if you carry a well of shame and unresolved trauma inside of you, no amount of money, no measure of success or celebrity can fill it."

It's true. Typically, that well of shame and unresolved trauma occurs during earliest childhood, from a variety of circumstances and often utterly unrealized by well-meaning parents. It is up to each of us to identify our own well of shame and unresolved trauma and set about resolving it. No one can truly love us and we cannot truly give love until this work occurs. The reward for doing this is huge. Imagine feeling impervious to comments and situations that used to leave you feeling gut sinks and knots. Imagine having thick enough skin that you can handle all sorts of drama and rejection with ease. This gives you the ability to fearlessly try all sorts of new things. It can happen and it is in your power.

How do you know what your attachment style is? There are several quizzes that can help reveal this. In a general way, if you want to be in a relationship but feel uncomfortable with it progressing, you may be avoidant. If you want someone in the same house as you but in a different room, you may be avoidant. If you want a partner but you only want to spend time with them on your terms, when you are finished with all the other items you need or want to get done, you may be avoidant. If you feel depressed when you think your partner may be checking out someone else, you may be anxious. If you often worry about what your partner is thinking or doing, you may be anxious. If you are constantly seeking reassurance, compliments, or validation from your partner, you may be anxious. If you often worry about your partner leaving you if they knew the real you, you may be anxious. The book *Attached* by Amir Levine and Rachel S.F. Heller states that one in four people, over a four-year period, are able to modify their attachment style from anxious or avoidant to stable, but this process does not come easily. It is one that requires great work and growth to develop a healthy self-view and view of others.

Even more interestingly, a person with a baseline anxious attachment style can find themselves become avoidant if they are paired with a person who is more anxiously attached than they are. Similarly, an avoidant person can become anxious if they are paired with someone more avoidant.

To further complicate the dating pool, there also exists a creature called the fearful avoidant. This person has a disorganized attachment style that is both highly anxious and avoidant. People with this attachment style want to be loved yet they make it an impossibility. They often come across as confident and capable, yet their fear of being hurt causes them to alternate between emotionally reactive and distant. This attachment style often occurs when the person's care providers become a source of fear to them. As a result, they crave love and are also massively scared to accept it.

How do these attachment styles happen? As infants, we are 100% dependent on our caregivers for food, safety, shelter, and emotional comfort. We learn through this process to trust them and to form a bond with them. If, however, the child experiences or perceives that the caretaker is not reliable or emotionally engaged, the child experiences extreme distress. One would think this distress would resolve as we grow to an age where we no longer rely on care providers for our survival. But it doesn't. The wound remains and we are continually attracted to situations that trigger it until we fully face and process through it.

That means if we are avoidant, we are attracted to those who are anxious. If we are anxious, we are attracted to those who are avoidant. These relationships are exciting and create the same neurochemistry we experienced as infants, which feels like "love" to us. It feels like home, even if home was a place that was a rollercoaster of pain and thrill. As an infant, even if our caregivers were unreliable, we experienced episodes where they were wonderful. As a result, we learned to crave those experiences. The rush of brain chemicals both from distress and being soothed became our "normal."

For most people, this type of childhood results in either an anxious or avoidant style. For a select few, it results in the extreme version of Disorganized Fearful/Avoidant. For the anxious style, the individual grows up always questioning whether they are good enough and lovable. They need frequent reassurance and validation from their partners. The avoidant grows up self-sufficient and independent. They learn they cannot depend on others, but they can depend on themselves. Although they crave connection, they value their space and control even more. They fear someone impinging on their safety and security. They fear being taken advantage of. They see relationships as work and burden, although they inherently still want them.

The avoidant will keep you at arm's length until you give up and leave, and then, and only then, feel an intense rush of feelings of love and intimacy they were unable to access before. If the partner returns, the avoidant experiences enormous relief but soon regresses to the previous distancing behavior, as keeping their partner at emotional distance is the only way they feel comfortable. A strategy an avoidant often subconsciously uses to achieve this is deactivating. One method of doing so is by focusing on the partner's negative qualities and behaviors to keep the partner at arm's length.

The avoidant person and the anxious person are both emotionally immature and they seek to bend people and circumstances to meet their will. The person who grows toward secure maturity seeks to understand, to collaborate, to love.

One of the most interesting things about both anxiously attached and avoidantly attached individuals is that they both struggle to say what they mean. Secure individuals are good at this, because they have emotional awareness and are not scared to say exactly how they feel. They have an expectation that if they do so, the other person will assist. Anxious and avoidant people are not experienced in this, and they also fear the outcome if they do it. They assume they will be rejected or abandoned. I catch myself in this every now and then. My teenager recently had several friends over for a late night get together and sleepover. They left pizza boxes everywhere upstairs. They stayed up until 3:45 am and the noise at times was waking me up. The next day I asked her a couple of times to clean up the pizza boxes. That night, she hadn't but promised she would. The next morning, on my way to work I walk into the kitchen and am greeted by a mound of pizza boxes on top of the kitchen trashcan. I felt a wave of anger. Relocating the boxes was not what I had in mind. I expected them to be put in the garage bin. Now, not only were they still an eyesore, but they were also preventing the kitchen trashcan from use.

I was angry and…something else…I couldn't put my finger on. I wanted to send an angry text about how disrespectful it was to delay taking care of this and then to not complete the job. On top of that, she and her friends staying up so late and being loud was inconsiderate, since they knew I had to be up early. As angry as I was, I fortunately did not send the text. I finally called her. Before I could say anything, she told me she had cleaned up the mess. I said, "No, you left the boxes on the trash." She said, "Yes, I did that last night and was planning to take them to the garage last night, but I forgot. I took care of it today." I was still angry. Then it dawned on me. Inside I felt hurt and angry and frustrated. But it wasn't because of pizza boxes or a noisy late night. It was because I missed her. She had started to spend all her free time with friends, rather than me or other adults. In addition to missing her, I was worried that she might be spending too much time with friends, and it could lead to trouble. I realized I had been thinking this in the back of my mind for a while. The hurt and fear bubbled into an anger wave that burst out over some pizza boxes. As soon as this dawned on me, the phone conversation quickly changed from one of finger pointing to an honest conversation where I admitted that I missed her, that I need more sleep and that I felt her social life was a bit too much to be healthy for her. We ended up agreeing that one night per week we would spend quality time together, just the two of us. We agreed on an activity for the first few weeks and left the call both very excited. A shift like that only takes seconds. A shift can leave both people feeling valued and inspired rather than feeling controlled or frustrated. Figure out what you are truly feeling, and then say what you mean. It is far easier to point fingers and be angry. The results you are looking for live in a place where you are honest, vulnerable, and brave.

It takes a great deal of introspection, counseling or coaching and mindfulness to become aware of why you are doing what you are doing but the rewards are so worth it. At the core, all insecure attachment styles stem from an inability to fully love and accept ourselves. When we do not love ourselves is when we are most likely to feel the need to dictate to others how they should love us. If we do not fully love ourselves, we tend to micromanage the way in which others love us. Rather than accept a significant other's particular style of showing love or affection, we find fault with it if it does not match our own style.

Love should be freely given in one's own unique way. Part of the fun of being loved is seeing how someone else uniquely shows you love, not dictating to them how it should be. Here is where I will take the controversial stance of challenging the love languages. I love the theory of the five love languages, and I love the idea of learning each other's love language. The five love languages are acts of service, words of affirmation, quality time, physical touch and receiving gifts. The theory is that we should put forth effort to learn what language most resonates with our partner and strive to primarily communicate love to them in that manner.

That said, my theory is that if we are so rigid that for us to feel properly loved, we must be spoken to only in our love language it seems to me we are being quite closed minded. If we truly love ourselves, we are already meeting our own love needs. What someone else gives us is their gift, their style, their interpretation. Do we want a machine, programmed to our specifications or do we want to experience someone else's unique personality and their way of showing love? I am a person who is very goal and task oriented. As a result, acts of service is the love language that most speaks to me. But if that is what I exclusively require from my lovers, how will I ever grow and develop? It would be like eating the same food every day of my life. No! The whole point of not being alone is being with someone who can show you parts of yourself you were less aware of. To grow and learn. To try new things. To venture out from our comfort zone.

I was once with a partner who was way different from me. I was type A and goal oriented. He was more passive and fun. My love language was acts of service. His were words of affirmation and physical touch. At the time, I had not yet learned about the love languages. My way of showing love was to complete projects that benefited him or us or the household. I worked hard at this. Despite all my hard-earned efforts, he never really felt loved. Because his love language was words of affirmation and physical touch, and I was providing less of those modalities, he felt deprived, even though my love for him was strong. Similarly, he gave me many words of affirmation and lots of physical touch which I often falsely interpreted as ingenuine and self-serving. In my mind flattery always had an agenda...as did physical touch. These things did not make me feel loved, they made me feel chased. As a result, I created more distance to get away from him. What I was looking for was acts of service. I wanted him to help me build a home and a future and an empire for future generations.

After we were apart, I learned about the five love languages. Our conflicts now made sense to me. I then convinced myself that what I needed was a man who was type A, goal oriented and, like me, found acts of service to be the most relevant love language. As luck would have it, I did find that person. And ironically enough, I soon began to miss having words of affirmation and physical touch. Life began to feel like a series of tasks and goals and business, with no real connection or change in scenery.

That is when I realized that although we think we want someone just like ourselves, we really do not thrive by being with our carbon copy. Differences are what make relationships exciting and fun. Even conflict, when handled well, builds intimacy. Two people who see eye to eye on everything make for a very boring and predictable dynamic.

So, if you find yourself attracted to someone who is emotionally much different than you, embrace it! Try to learn as much as you can about why they are the way they are. Instead of judging them for being different from you, focus on curiosity and empathy. Ask them questions. Learn what they feel and what is going on in their mind to accompany their feelings. It can be a fascinating journey that will help both of you grow and will deepen your intimacy and connection.

The degree to which someone likes us is rarely tied to how attractive, smart, successful, or stylish we are. It is tied to how we make them feel. How do we make others feel? In breakups we tend to feel a crushed ego tied to thinking that we weren't enough. But what if it wasn't that we were not enough, but rather it was that we never made them feel as though they were enough?

In times of relationship challenges, people often struggle with the choice of whether to stay or leave. It can be incredibly confusing. Mostly it is confusing because we hinge the decision on whether the other person will change. Since we can never "make" someone else change, the better strategy is this:

First, stop pointing the finger (at least for a minute!) and look within. Am I showing up in this relationship as my best self? The self that the other person wants and needs, not just the one that is comfortable for me to be? Sometimes we are self-righteously indignant that we are doing all the heavy lifting in the relationship without stopping to realize we are only lifting the bags we want to lift. In what ways are we contributing to the relationship? Are they ways that even matter to the other person? Or are they ways that happen to be tied to our own values and priorities?

I see this a lot in relationships. Women often complain that they "take care of everything" around the house, without realizing that this is really because the things they are doing are not particularly important to a man. If, as partners, we first take time to see what is important to the other person, and reprioritize our "tasks", even temporarily, sometimes it makes all the difference. Once we become curious about the other person's needs, and attempt to meet those needs, it becomes much easier to ask them to meet our needs.

CHAPTER 16

The Five Factors for Feeling Full

Never in our history have we seen so much anxiety and depression, suicide, and substance abuse. Why? What has changed?

Our world is moving fast and some of the ways we formerly met core emotional needs no longer inherently exist in our way of life. How do we meet them now? Part of the process of becoming truly empathetic is to learn to self-care and self-love until we are full. How do we do that?

1) Connections

We fundamentally require connection to ourselves, to a higher purpose and to others. Until recently, large families throughout history lived close together and engaged in a wide variety of connecting activities like reunions, dinners, rituals, and traditions. Today's fast-paced technology-dependent world is simply different. Effective new methods of human connection will eventually catch up with our modern life. We are getting there, but meanwhile, on an individual level there is some work to do.

Self-awareness time connecting with yourself and your higher purpose, whatever version of that fits you. This is a key ingredient in developing your most authentic self. The you that knows your path, your value, and your purpose. This step involves fully feeling and working through all emotions, even your negative emotions. This can happen through meditation, journaling, walks in nature, yoga, purposeful deep breathing or any method that helps you stop, release your thoughts, fully feel and open yourself to deeper awareness. Historically, people did this somewhat effortlessly, by lifestyle and societal culture.

Now that we have 24/7 information and entertainment at our fingertips, it has become much easier to look out than in.

Spending effort and time in meaningful connection with others. This means not waiting for others to come to you. (They probably won't, they are too busy on their phones!) It means understanding your value (developed from the first step) and then reaching out to build others up, without fear of rejection and without expectation of return. It is not about the response from them. It is about you growing and expanding. Over time, these deposits into your emotional bank pay off in a big way.

2) Fuel

Because we are housed in a physical body, we are governed by physical limitations. As a result, we feel optimum mental and emotional stability when our nutrition and sleep are on point. Athletes know peak performance requires solid fueling habits, including the right food, supplements, sleep, inspiration, and relaxation time. The last fifty years have seen an enormous increase in readily available processed fast foods, foods that do our mental or emotional health no favors.

About a decade ago, I was introduced by a friend to Rockstar Juiced orange juice energy drink. Caffeine was my one vice, and it did not take me long to be hooked! On a day-by-day basis I thought it made me better. When I look back years later, it did not. What it did was make me reactive, impatient, and impulsive. Over the years, it affected my hormones and skin. It reduced my ability to be intimate and vulnerable in relationships and did extensive damage relationally. I was always in 100 percent go mode and that is not a healthy place to be. In recent years, I have gradually reduced my caffeine intake to minimal and I feel much more serene. I can engage and feel the moment. Ironically, I am more effective at work and more productive in general. I am no longer exhausted at night.

The relationship between sugar and well-being cannot be denied. Sugar causes our body to require more minerals – minerals most of us already do not get nearly enough of. Deficiencies in certain minerals can have drastic effects on our nervous system and can contribute to insomnia, anxiety, panic disorder, and depression.

The point is this. What we eat, read, watch, and listen to impacts us. Fuel well to feel well.

3) Energy Release

We are energetic beings. Think of a horse racing around a pasture right before a storm. Can you imagine if the horse stuffed those feelings and stood still despite how he felt inside? Picture the aggression that comes from a dog that has spent time on a chain in a backyard. Modern life is sedentary, causing us to stuff and ignore our energy. We are usually the spectator, rather than the participant. All of that pent up energy leads to anxiousness, restlessness and discontent.

Exercise, outdoor sports, dancing, playing with kids, going out with friends, laughing, crying, screaming, and singing at the top of your lungs are all great ways to release and let go!

4) Awareness

Purposeful learning leads to awareness. As children, we are sponges. Endlessly curious, open to possibilities, eager to take it all in. The happiest, most productive people nurture and feed their inner spark to learn and grow. Because of this they are never bored, no matter their environment.

In centuries past, education and learning were highly valued and respected. What happens to our emotional health when we spend more time-consuming mental cotton candy than in searching for profound insight? We are seeing the answer.

Traveling, reading, going to conferences, hiring a coach or counselor, trying new experiences, and learning new skills are solid ways to kickstart insight and fire up your life.

5) Challenge

We are wired for struggle. We crave it. So much so, that when life is too easy, we are miserable. Without realizing it, we subconsciously create chaos and drama, especially relationship and financial drama, as an outlet simply to feel alive. Our biological need for this is real. Channeling it into something constructive is the key. Incredible fulfillment comes from accepting challenges and experiencing struggle. The pain you feel from doing something hard makes you feel alive. Pushing past our limits for a solid purpose is a rush like no other.

We all have modern life stressors but most of us have enough to eat, a warm bed, toilet facilities and minimal imminent danger of being decapitated by warriors or wild animals.

In decades past, children, for the sake of family survival, had to work long hours on farms and in family businesses. Now they are "busy" with dance classes, concerts, and gymnastics. These are good things that follow progress, but these activities fail to bring the same sense of purpose as knowing the family is relying on you for the survival of the unit. *To some extent, along our journey of progress, we've lost some of our innate soul charging challenge.* In a subconscious search for it, we run up our credit cards, pick fights with our spouses, become mean girls in high school and generally cause ourselves drama.

The real point of progress is to free people up from the tasks of survival, so they can collectively solve more universal problems.

Progress has achieved its goal. At the same time, societal anxiety, depression, and substance abuse have risen at the same pace that the elements we used to rely on to keep us "human" have fallen out of our lifestyle. Building back in elements to meet our core emotional needs takes purposeful work, but as the rate of opioid overdoses, suicides, anxiety, and depression skyrocket, it is clear the stakes have never been higher.

I'm a runner. I started running in my 20's to lose weight and I hated it. But I made myself. Now I run 100-mile ultramarathons, I have a tremendous running community friend group, and without a doubt it has changed my life in a thousand miraculous ways.

As a result, nothing triggers me more than someone weakly smiling at me and saying "Oh, it's so amazing what you do. I wish I could like running."

Do people actually think I find running more pleasurable than their choice activities of shopping, watching movies and eating out? Because I assure you, I do not.

It's not "fun." It's a matter of grit and discipline. It's a matter of personal responsibility to be my best every day.

I run because when we require ourselves to repeatedly do hard physical things, our brains work better, our moods are more stable, our creativity comes alive, and our positivity is regenerated.

So would I like to lounge around and gain weight? Would it be more fun than cold, dark, rainy, gut-wrenching runs? Sure.

But every aspect of my life is better because I require myself to include physical effort in my day. It makes me a better friend, partner, employee, and boss.

By all means, you, you person who "wishes" you could like running, go on and keep taking that path of least resistance, doing only the things that feel good to you. You will likely never feel the thrill of accomplishing your dreams, the power of creative new thoughts, the energy to carry them through. But by all means, go back to your Cheetos and Netflix, since it's so much easier to "like" those. Maybe someday you'll wake up and magically like to run.

Making the choice to embrace the hard path leads to fulfillment and self-confidence and the ability to inspire others.

How can you stay consistent, even when you do not feel like running? You can life hack it. Over the years I have developed many accountable friends in running. We all push each other by continually inviting each other for runs. Socialization and companionship make the hardship of the run tolerable, even fun. I sign up for races. Something about having a race on my calendar, with a daily training plan to go with it, keeps me on track. It then becomes a part of my mandatory routine, just like brushing my teeth and going to work. I almost never "want" to go do those workouts but the way I feel after is priceless. The way my blood flows through my veins is simply different when I'm training than when I'm not. It feels good. It feels alive. Humans were wired for challenge. Without it we feel lost.

Character and grit mean challenging yourself to do the hard thing when you don't want to. It's the magical place where self-esteem and self-confidence are born.

Push yourself to do hard things, look for ways to learn and grow. There is a saying that only boring people get bored. It's true! If you open your eyes to all the possibilities around you, to learn, to develop and to do, you will never be bored.

Remember, you don't get what you deserve in this life. You get what you fight for.

It's eating the tuna instead of the chocolate.
It's running when it's cold and rainy.
It's saying I forgive you when you're angry.
It's cold-calling sales leads when you know you'll hear "no."
It's training when you have no race on the books.

It's where the magic begins.

CHAPTER 17

The Hardest Things are also the Easiest

TYPICALLY THE EASIEST PATHS LEAD TO THE HARDEST LIVES, AND the hardest paths lead to the easiest lives.

Years ago, I remember being in law school and working as a nurse. I was a single mother at the time, and I remember frequently being judged by my peers and those older than me. They told me I should not pursue law school, that it would be too hard as a single mother, that I should just work as a nurse and spend more time with my child. Really? The fact is it wasn't that hard. It was a matter of time blocking and time management. It was a matter of being purposeful with my time. It was a matter of including my daughter in as many aspects of my education as possible, to maximize our time together.

I told those who judged me that, yes, it might be tough for a season. For three years. But the payoff would change her life forever. The experiences, lifestyle and connections she would have forever because of me pursuing my abilities rather than stifling them would be priceless for both of us.

The truth is time is a trade-off. I did not have less time with her than my peers had with their children. I had a different type of time with her. While they were watching TV with their kids, my child was in my lap helping me highlight passages in law briefs. While they were sitting idly watching their kids do gymnastics practice, I was watching her gymnastics practice with headphones in my ears, listening to study guides. While we were on road trips, we were listening to class notes, rather than the radio. Do you think my daughter knew the difference? No. We joke now that we went to law school together. She practically became the law school mascot. She had as many law students at her birthday parties as she did her friends. Was her life different? Yes. In my mind, it was as good or better, probably infinitely better, than had I simply worked as a nurse the rest of her life. Not because being a lawyer is better than being a nurse. It's not. But pursuing your natural gifts and maximum abilities is always better…. every single time.

Those three years that started when she was 3 years old massively changed the rest of her life. It changed where we lived, my work schedule, my income, my friends, her friends. It changed who I married. It changed everything. For the better. It changed my confidence, my parenting skills, my vision for both who I could become and who she could become. It was a decision that was hard but was also the easiest. Now, in my 40's am I glad? Infinitely so. Is she glad? More than infinitely so! Barriers are only there to the extent we allow them. Often you do not have to exclusively choose between one thing and another. You can have both if you methodically and purposefully plan how.

The fact is, after I finished law school, my life became infinitely easier and more family friendly than it had ever been as a nurse. I went from working nights and weekends and having an unpredictable schedule to working Monday through Friday. I went from working grueling 12-hour shifts that made me exhausted to working a reasonable 8 hour day. I went from being stressed about what to do with my life, to feeling good that I was doing it. After law school, we spent almost every weekend traveling and adventuring. I made more money as a lawyer, and we had the funds to enjoy life. Because my schedule was more predictable, we could plan many trips. I had more energy because the work I did was less physically demanding. Three hard years led to a lifetime of easier years. That is usually how it works. Buckle down for the short term and reap the rewards forever.

In my late 20's I began running. I ran casual 5k's and 10k's and it truly changed my life and outlook. I had "run a marathon" on my bucket list simply because it seemed impossible to me and I liked the adrenaline rush of chasing the impossible. I joined the Leukemia and Lymphoma society Team in Training because it seemed the only realistic way to get through training for a full marathon. I'll never forget that first meeting. Listening to the coach talk about what we were signing up for made me feel incredible. Like a real athlete. Like we were somehow elite. It was exciting and intimidating all in one. I remember prior to this thinking how on earth do people run long distances? I hated running! One mile in I was usually toast…and bored out of my mind.

Joining that group was one of the most influential decisions of my life. We met as a group every Saturday morning and I remember being amazed at how no one in the group ever complained. Ever. If it was cold, rainy, windy, it didn't matter. They were smiling and uplifting and encouraging. I was amazed. Over time a 5 mile ran became easy. Then a 10-mile run. Each run became a fun social experience of chatting and laughing. As I became more conditioned, the miles began to easily fly by. I looked forward all week to Saturday morning. That group of gritty runners got me through my first marathon. At the end of the marathon, I remember feeling like I might faint, and I wasn't sure what my name was. I thought to myself, "check…ran a marathon…will never do this again."

For the next few years, I continued running 5k's, 10K's and an occasional half-marathon.

Then I moved to Birmingham, Alabama, home of one of the most active trail running and road running communities in the nation. The first time I went hiking in one of the local hilly wooded state parks, I remember huffing and puffing. Then I saw trail runners glide by. I was stunned. They RUN this??? I could not even fathom running up mountains dodging tree roots and rocks. I was struggling just to walk it.

One day I saw a colleague in my office limp into work on a Monday morning. I asked her why she was limping. She grinned from ear to ear and said she had been training for the Grand Canyon stage race. "What?" I asked. She then told me how she was training for a race that would involve running 170 miles over several days, carrying a backpack and camping each night. I was intrigued. She was limping because over the weekend she had run 25 miles of hilly wooded trails on Saturday with a 15-pound backpack and 20 miles on Sunday. This, I could not wrap my brain around. How could an average looking person do this? I pondered it. We kept in touch, and I watched her train.

One year later we went to lunch. She said, "I'm thinking about running the world's most dangerous endurance race. It's called Jungle Marathon and it's in Brazil. It's eighteen months from now. It's running 157 miles in 7 days with everything you need for the week in a backpack on your back. We'll be climbing mountains and swimming rivers and lakes and trudging through swamps. Want to join?"

My first thought? This is not possible for me. At the time I was running 10-15 miles a week on roads. My second thought was, "Yes, but you also did not think you could run a marathon. And you did."

I looked at her and with all the conviction of an utterly naïve wanna-be athlete, I said, "yes."

Tim Ferris, in his book *The 4-Hour Workweek*, says doing the unrealistic is easier than the realistic. He says "It's lonely at the top. 99% of the world is convinced they are incapable of achieving great things, so they aim for the mediocre middle ground. The level of competition is thus fiercest for "realistic" goals, paradoxically making them the most time and energy consuming."

I completely agree. When I ran my marathon, I competed against tens of thousands of runners. I did not have the slightest chance of being even in the top 25%. When I ran the 157 mile Jungle Marathon in Brazil, I was competing against 40 people from 14 countries. Of those 40 people, half did not finish. I finished 5th female.

What I learned from the Jungle Marathon was that shooting for a goal so seemingly unattainable turned me into a different person. Once I committed, people and resources flocked around me. I hired a coach. My training, nutrition and focus became locked in. Training for those eighteen months became the best period of my life. My body and my mind underwent a complete evolution. I became leaner, faster, stronger. More decisive, more disciplined, more confident. I felt better than I ever had in my entire life.

Setting such a high goal caused people to continually ask me about my training, support me and encourage me. This doesn't happen when you set a mediocre goal. As a result, staying on track for the Jungle Marathon was easy. I felt I had throngs of people pushing me and holding me accountable. I was carried on the waves of their enthusiasm. I was high on life every day. People were watching to see if I could do it. It was all very inspiring and humbling and lifechanging. I was a very average, mediocre runner at the beginning of those eighteen months. By the end I felt like a real athlete for the first time in my life.

Setting extremely high goals, committing to them, and then telling your people to hold your feet to the fire is the way to embark on a journey you will never regret. It is how you become a better version of yourself than you ever thought you could be.

Doing that very hard thing suddenly made everything else in my life seem easy. Sitting at my desk on Monday mornings was heaven, after being bruised, battered, bitten, dehydrated, exhausted in the Amazon jungle. It gave me perspective and gratitude about all the average things in my life. It made me more present and this in turn made my life infinitely richer.

Average minded people will tell you law school or med school or starting a business or becoming a CEO "take too long" or "are too hard." Guess what? Working as a laborer or in a job you do not like for 40 years is infinitely harder than spending 10 years gaining education and skill to do something incredibly rewarding, both financially and intellectually. Working at a dead-end job for 40 years will drain your spirit and health. Working your way toward your natural abilities, investing in yourself, looking long term will bring exhilaration to your life.

Will working your way up rather than sideways be harder at times? Certainly. For a season. And then it will be easier in the long term.

Training for the Jungle Marathon was incredibly hard for eighteen months. What I learned and developed made the rest of my runs and physical fitness for years to come incredibly easy.

Sometimes the hardest things are not what you would think would be hard.

I am a very Type A, adrenaline seeking personality type. My oldest daughter is my opposite. She is very good at being. I am anxious unless I am "doing." She is creative. I was, until recent years, not. She was thoughtful and reflective. I was brash and full throttle.

During her teen years, she morphed from being a joyful "full of life" extroverted child to becoming withdrawn and quiet. She slept a lot and spent a lot of time alone. She became less motivated and almost apathetic.

As any well-meaning mis-informed type A parent would, I set about trying to "fix" her. I assumed in my ignorant arrogance that my busy lifestyle was "right" and her slow pace was "wrong."

I didn't know or understand at that time that she was suffering from anxiety and depression. I just knew she was not doing what I thought she should be. This mismatch of expectations and performance caused a great deal of friction between us. The more I pushed, the more she retreated. The more I gave rah rah speeches and threatened loss of privileges, the more she became sad and quiet.

Her lounging around in bed when I felt she should be productive caused me great triggers. I would become angry, scared, frustrated. I often took it out on her verbally, which I now regret. I would verbally assault her, only to lay in bed at night hurting and feeling massive anxiety because I knew what I was doing wasn't the right path. I didn't know what the right path was. I simply wanted her to be okay. I wanted us both to be okay.

After one particularly difficult day where she laid around most of the day, we had a blow up. She retreated to her room, I retreated to my work. Something in my heart kept screaming at me. Go to her. GO TO HER. And do what, I thought? She is being a defiant and lazy teenager. I am right to be harsh with her. To motivate her. She had a great childhood. She has no right or reason to be like this. "No," the voice said. "You're wrong." I felt an incredible inner battle. A war between my ego, my fear, and my love for my daughter. I kept hearing the voice. GO TO HER. I couldn't go to her. I was paralyzed. I had never been good at being vulnerable or talking about emotions. In fact, I was woefully inadequate at it. Work made me feel good. Telling others what to do made me feel good. Talking about feelings gave me massive anxiety.

I fought myself for at least 10 minutes. I was utterly terrified to walk into her room and do the one thing I knew I needed to do. Finally, I did it.

I walked into her room. She was curled up on her bed in a sad fetal position. I climbed onto her bed and sat cross legged. I took her hands in mine. I looked into her eyes. I said, "I can see that you have pain inside. I do not understand exactly why, and I don't know whether you will ever be comfortable sharing it with me. But know that I am here, and I love you and I support you and we are going to get through this." Her eyes glistened. Her shoulders relaxed. She never said a word.

That was the beginning of an utter transformation in our relationship. We went from strained to supportive. Uncertain to grounded. Anxious to safe.

It became easier. That one hard thing that took 2 excruciating minutes turned into years of powerful bond and deeper love that I could ever have imagined.

We may think we know what is going on with someone else, but odds are we do not. It was not for me to judge her behavior. It was my place to have compassion and curiosity. To support, not admonish. To create a safe place for her to heal.

Though I did not know it at the time, she DID have intense pain. Pain she was not able to share with me at that time. I had been judging her lack of motivation without the slightest insight into her pain.

Today I am unbelievably proud of the person she has become. I look at her in awe. She is not the miniature version of me I once tried to mold. She is her. She is very different than me and in the best possible way. She is beyond amazing to me.

Choose to do the hard thing. The thing you hear inside you to do. The thing you want to turn away from because it is hard. Turn toward it.

Turning to the flip side, what happens if you choose to do the easy thing, the thing that feels good? Usually, although not always, the feel good, "do what I want to" path leads to a scarred and traumatic life.

Affairs are a classic example of this. Substance abuse is another. Think about Tiger Woods. At the pinnacle of his career, he could have and get anything he wanted. The power went to his head, and he began acting on all the easy temptations all around him. It was easy and it felt good. He felt powerful and became arrogant. Fast forward a couple years and his entire life and career came crashing down around him. It took many years to come back and he will always be known as the guy who let his weaknesses get the best of him, causing him to lose a beautiful wife and family and a rock-solid career.

A few years ago, I had a doctor friend who was truly an outstanding physician. She was unbelievable talented, compassionate, driven, and focused. She had a booming practice and her patients adored her. She mentored many other physicians and nurses and was well respected by all. Her life was disciplined and structured, certainly, but also incredibly fulfilling and well rewarded. In her 50's she went through a divorce. Something about that process changed something in her. It was as though she lost her strength and centered mindset.

She began missing work, showing up on an erratic schedule. She made some reckless business decisions that caused her further stress and work requirements. She found a boyfriend in another state and began spending all her free time traveling to see him. She barely spent time with her children, lost the respect of her peers and began losing clients. She lost all the anchors of her life by choosing to follow the "feel good" thing at the expense of her life responsibilities.

Fast forward a year and the boyfriend broke up with her, the children barely spoke to her, her practice was almost non-existent. The "feel-good, easy, self-indulgent" path usually leads to heartache and a hard life.

In her case, it is possible that "limerence" played a role. Limerence, also, often referred to as a "crush" can be defined as an involuntary state of intense romantic desire, often triggered by the heady cocktail of chemicals that arise in a new relationship. It can be characterized by ruminative thinking, anxiety and depression, temporary fixation, and the disintegration of self. This arises when the subject of desire is hot and cold, causing unattainability. This unreasoned, often un-fully realized love can rise to a type of unhealthy addiction that can cause utter ruin. It feels like the "right" thing. Your brain says it's your only choice. But it may be oh so wrong.

What do we do to prevent falling down easy street and heading for hardship? The reality is our brains are not always reliable sources of advice. Sometimes neither is our hearts. This is why we absolutely need accountability in our lives. We need mentors, coaches, parents, strong friends, pastors, teachers, counselors, doctors. These invaluable individuals give us perspective. Just like teenagers sometimes act impulsively and ignore risks, sometimes adults do as well, especially after a traumatic event or when in the throes of a new potential relationship. It is critical to have sounding boards in your life, sounding boards who know your values and goals and hold you steadfast to them. It is simply too easy for ANY of us to fall into temptation of what looks like opportunity or bliss and, in the process, lose all the things in our life that matter most. As my mother always said, "pride goes before a fall." If you feel your life has become too good to be true, it might be.

Typically, when we "do what we want," we miss out on "being what we could be." Over-indulgence rarely ends well. When we show up late to work and leave early, we miss out on the big opportunities. It also weakens our character, which undermines our self-confidence.

When we eat whatever we want we end up being unhappy with how our body looks and how it performs for us. We may end up tired, cranky, overweight, and unmotivated. When we stay up all night watching TV, we may end up accomplishing nothing the next day and have feelings of self-loathing and guilt due to missed opportunities and, once again, erosion of character and self-confidence.

Choosing to exercise grit by choosing the hard thing builds self-confidence and leads to big opportunities. Few people are willing to choose to do the hard thing. Those who do stand out. They become our leaders.

We are not here to be continually comforted, entertained, and indulged. We are here to face adversity, make difficult choices, rise above situations and evolve into higher level beings. We are here to serve, to help, to love and to grow.

We are not here to continually receive, respond and react. We are also here to do and create and provide.

There is an old saying, "if you do not stand for something, you will fall for anything." Stand for choosing the path that leads to being all you can be. Evaluate every decision, every temptation under that framework.

Does the decision lead to you becoming the best human you can possibly be? Does it lead to you being a better friend, significant other, spouse, parent, sibling, or employee? Does it lead to you being able to give more? Does it lead to you challenging yourself and rising in a way that will later help others more? If not, walk the other way, even if it does not feel as good, even if it is not what you want to do.

We are seeing a new trend with employees. Some employees appreciate the overall mission of a company, appreciate their role in it and will roll up their sleeves and do whatever is needed to accomplish that mission. More frequently though I see employees who are rigidly attached to their job description and refuse to do anything outside of that. Having personal pride and a customer service attitude that is willing to go the extra mile and be a part of the mission, rather than just a person collecting a paycheck, really changes personal job satisfaction. I rarely see the former type of employee experience "burn out" even though they often work harder. I frequently see the second type of employee burn out. If your focus is simply to collect a paycheck, you will lack excitement and enthusiasm for your workday. If you can see the bigger picture and be willing to evolve in your role and participate wherever there is a need, you will automatically enjoy your workday more and, concurrently, you will likely have more opportunities come your way.

The universe migrates towards those who have gratitude, enthusiasm, and willingness to put forth effort under any circumstance. Effort is everything.

It's not easy to consistently put forth effort. None of us have discipline all the time. None of us have perspective all the time. It is surprisingly easy for even the best of us to fall into entitled or jealous or unengaged mindsets. Working hard, staying mindful, exercising, eating healthy do not always feel good or seem appealing. You know what does feel good? A quart of ice cream, a bottle of wine, a shopping spree, a drug, an affair. Can you trust those "feel good" feelings? Certainly not. What "feels" right is usually the easy path, not the rewarding, fulfilling higher road path. But what feels easy now becomes a very hard path later. What feels too difficult now often becomes an amazing result later. It's worth it, every time.

KNOWING

How do you know which part of your intuition and feelings to trust and which part will lead you astray? The fact is, sometimes you won't. That is why creating accountability all around your life is so critical. Surround yourself with people who will be honest with you and who will "check" you. Place boundaries and accountability in your life in all areas before the temptation is there. Decide before you go out how much alcohol you will drink and why you are going to stop there. Fix that in your brain BEFORE you experience the temptation and peer pressure of the environment. Create a "why" behind it. Do this for every area of your life where you may be tempted to slack or stray.

When I was training for the Amazon jungle race, my why was that I feared falling behind the other runners, especially during the night runs, and potentially being lost forever or attacked by jaguars. It was a powerful why. I kept it fixed in my mind for 18 months of training and I almost never missed a long run. Your why is the factor that will keep you on track when you are feeling weak-minded.

Once you establish accountability boundaries in your life, also build in some reasonable "slack." No one can be rigidly disciplined all the time, nor should we be. Plan in some indulgences and grace here and there to reward your effort. Find balance. Studies have shown that no human can maintain constant discipline in all areas of life. If you are overly disciplined in your career, fitness, and finance, you may falter in your relationship. Maintaining willpower requires a high degree of mental energy. Build in mental relaxation and indulgence so you can stay on track most of the time.

When we do stray from who we want to be, it is often because we lose track of our knowing, our thinking or our feeling. Sometimes even when we do think and feel something is wrong, we still do it. We feel a desire to do something and then think thoughts that rationalize our desire. We then block out the feeling of "knowing" it is wrong and proceed.

A great example is an affair. If the cheater felt it was wrong and thought about how wrong it was, they would not do it. The reality is, our heart and mind trick us into thinking it is okay. Deep within us is still the "knowing" that it is wrong, that it is a lie and that it is not who we are, yet we listen to the heart and mind and proceed down a path that leads to great harm. It is very hard to overcome the two-pronged motivation of a temptation that both feels good and has been rationalized in the mind.

So how do you know? Where people often get confused in an affair is the feeling part. They decide it feels right therefore it must be right. They think "What if this person is supposed to become the love of my life?" This confuses them because it feels like a path they should proceed down. How do you know which voice to listen to? Your heart, your mind or your gut?

When you feel confused as to what thoughts or feelings to trust, try this. Keep in mind the differences between knowing, thinking, and feeling. Of the three, knowing is the most reliable guide. In your gut you "know" certain things. You know it is wrong to have an affair, regardless of the circumstances. You know it is wrong to sleep at work. You know it is wrong to lie. If we know that, why do even the best of us sometimes slip and do the wrong thing? Why did Tiger Woods, a talented golfer, get swept up into a cycle of repeated infidelity? Because we forget sometimes to listen to our "knowing." We feel the pull of desire. We then begin thinking our way into a justification to do it. If we block out our "knowing," soon the thinking and feeling take over. We create a whole scenario of reasons in our mind why it is ok to give into this feeling of desire. "I need this ice cream tonight because I feel worn down. The calcium will be good for me." "I deserve this fun day with this person I'm attracted to because my significant other no longer gives me enough attention." "It's okay to lie this time because it is for an important reason, and it will not hurt anyone."

Our brain and our feelings are not always trustworthy. Our knowing is. When we meditate, when we pray, when we tune into our bodies and feel the tension and listen to it, we know what we need to do. We feel the craving for the drug or the alcohol or the ice cream but if we stop and really assess the craving and breathe and feel everything in our body, we will know there is something better we can eat to fuel our beautiful bodies. We will then have the willpower to overcome our thinking and feeling and do the right thing.

The next time you feel compelled to walk down a questionable path or reach for something that causes you to stray from who you want to be, try this exercise:

Close your eyes and in your heart feel the desire. Acknowledge it. Try to find out what the heart is truly needing and asking for. Is it really this thing? Or is this thing a convenient band aid? Is it peer pressure? Could it hurt someone or yourself? Go to your mind and see if you are creating excuses and justifications. If so, you are likely on a road that is straying from your authentic core. Next go to your gut.

Remind yourself what kind of person you are determined to become. Honest, trustworthy, reliable, productive, kind, generous, purposeful, confident? Now ask yourself if this choice brings you closer to that or farther. Ask yourself if others knew what you were doing, how would they view you? Why would they view you that way?

Now you know. Your knowing, when developed, is your way to keep your thinking and feeling in check.

WALKING WOUNDED

Sometimes, to do the hard things that lead to fulfillment, we must spend a period of time walking wounded. Many of the most fulfilling, exciting, meaningful things in life come at the price of great sacrifice.

I recently learned how to swim. I mean, I knew how to swim. Sort of. As a teen, I taught myself how to swim because my parents had never taken any of us kids to swim lessons. I was frustrated and embarrassed that I was the only kid at pool parties that did not know how to swim, so around the age of 14, I determined to teach myself how. Fortunately for me, my father had a short-term travel assignment that required us to live in an apartment with a pool for the summer. I went to the pool every day and slowly taught myself to float, doggie paddle and eventually swim. I was still scared of the water and had a few close calls that left me spooked but I at least I became competent at birthday pool parties.

Over the years, I became reasonably adept at what I call "Tarzan swimming," meaning, swimming free style with my head up. For the last 5 years or so I badly wanted to do a triathlon but my inability to swim with my face in the water was a handicap. I knew I could never swim efficiently with my head up, and therefore would never be able to swim a significant distance. For years, my running friends would ask if I wanted to join them for a short triathlon. I always sadly shook my head "no" and said, "I am not a good enough swimmer." One day about a year ago I had said those words one too many times. I was angry. "WHY am I not a good swimmer," I thought to myself? Just because my parents did not provide me with this skill did not mean I could not pay for it myself. I was determined to quit making excuses and choose to do something hard, something way outside my comfort zone.

I paid for a swim coach and began learning how to swim using rhythmic breathing. It was truly one of the hardest skills I have ever learned. I fought every drop of it. The water constantly leaked into my goggles, up my nose or down my throat. I was flailing and gasping. My goggles were fogging and leaking. I would swim about 10 yards and then stop, hyperventilating and coughing. I felt like the biggest loser. What was wrong with me?? I talked to other people. Did they have this problem? They looked at me blankly. Truth be told, they probably did, but when you learn to swim as a 4-year-old, you forget the traumatic aspects of the journey. I continued. After a few lessons, I kept practicing on my own, trying to master what I had learned. I hated every session. I hated that the chlorine was destroying my hair, that my goggles gave me raccoon eye bags, that I had a continual post-nasal drip from inhaled water. I was embarrassed that the other smooth, graceful swimmers at the Y were laughing at this determined swimmer who likely resembled an angry octopus during her weekly attempt at laps.

But I kept at it. Over time, my ability to swim longer distances without stopping to catch up with my breath improved. I learned to pre-condition my hair before a swim to prevent chlorine destruction. I learned they made Femme goggles for women with small faces. I learned which anti-fog spray to use. It was slow, painful progress but it was in fact progress. I dreaded those first 20 or so swims but eventually it became very tolerable. I started to feel I was really making progress. One day, two weeks before my first scheduled Olympic triathlon,

I finally went to a lake to see if my skills were adequate for a true triathlon experience. I was sure I could do it. Unfortunately, the result turned out to be devastating.

In the pool, I would often stop at the end and collect myself. I did this every few laps. Catching my breath and just standing there for a minute. The moment my torso entered the cold, deep lake water, I felt all my muscles tense. I put my face in and rather than the clear pool water and neatly painted black line, I saw green murk. Panic swelled over me. I forced myself to calm down and began my stroke, breathing to the right every few strokes as I always had. Within 200 yards I was gasping for breath. I stopped and held onto a kayak near me and collected myself. When I set out again, the same thing happened. I was scared, angry, cold, and out of breath. I was also panicked that this clearly meant I would not be able to survive my upcoming race.

I went home and wallowed in self-pity for a while. Clearly there was something wrong with me. Other people did not have this level of difficulty with swimming. What was my problem? Was I broken? Too rigid? Lacking the grace and calm that swimming required? Would I never be able to do it?

I texted a few friends who had done triathlons. One offered to swim with me at a pool the next day. I accepted. That morning I was nervous. She was a great swimmer. Would she be appalled at my lack of ability? Laugh that I was naive enough to sign up for an event that included a one-mile swim in a lake, when I had never successfully swum in a lake before?

I stuffed my anxiety into an internal bottle and screwed the cap on tight. I met her at the pool attempting to feel confident. She gave me a few pointers but was not able to fully assess what was causing me to run out of breath and stop so frequently. We practiced strokes and mechanics and it helped somewhat. She taught me to breathe on every stroke, taking small sips of air instead of the lion gasps I had grown accustomed to.

The next day I went back to my pool. I attempted to practice what I had learned. Prior to her showing me the "breathe every stroke" method, I had thought I was doing a "breathe every three strokes" method. I even counted. "Breathe, 1,2,3, breathe, 1,2,3." My method was causing my lungs to hurt. Her method of every stroke was causing me to not always be able to clear my head above the water. I was sucking down tons of water. Both methods had me in tears. At the end of the pool, I saw two older men sitting in chairs watching me. I had seen them swim many times. Both were effortlessly beautiful swimmers. Barely a ripple of water emanated out from their lean bodies gliding through the water. They must be dying laughing, I thought to myself as I struggled to lift my head out of the water to breathe every stroke. I finally finished my 30 minutes and climbed out. I plopped down by my things, which happened to be by one of the older men. He smiled kindly at me and asked how I was doing.

I looked at him sadly and said, "I'm trying to learn how to swim." He laughed. He said, "You looked like you were swimming fine to me, what's the problem?" I explained my dilemma. I needed to be able to swim a mile without stopping. In choppy cold lake water with people thrashing all around me. Without running out of breath. Which was something I currently could not even muster after 4 or 5 laps in a serene pool.

He asked me what my current breathing pattern was. I told him every three strokes. I then said, "I also need to learn to breathe to the left because currently I only breathe to the right and in a triathlon, I need to be competent at breathing on both sides. He started laughing again. I looked at him curiously. He winked and said, "if you are breathing every three strokes, how are you breathing on the right side every time." I stared at him blankly. What? Wait…" breathe, 1,2,3, breathe." Holy moly. He was right. I slapped my forehead. All along I had been breathing every FOURTH stroke, not every three. No wonder I never had enough air. No wonder I was trying to roll on my side to have time to suck down a lion size gulp of air. It all made sense now!

I got back in the water. The first few times I tried to breathe to the left were extremely awkward. I had to raise my head up high to turn it and clear. And then, suddenly it was like magic. The fact that I started breathing on both sides caused me to automatically employ more body rotation with my strokes. This in turn gave me more glide and made it easier to breathe without raising my head from the water. No longer raising my head up to breathe made my swimming easier. Breathing every three strokes instead of every four made a world of difference in terms of no longer feeling perpetually winded. And just like that I became a swimmer. I went from feeling utterly defeated and worthless to feeling like a champ. All because I continued to strive, even when I was embarrassingly non-proficient. I walked wounded until I could walk well. I asked for help. That's the real key. I cannot say enough about this one life hack. Ask for help. Every time. You are human and you have likely only been around a few decades. You are not going to know it all. If you want to hack your way to success much quicker, and shed the emotional baggage of feeling inadequate, start asking for help, for advice and for tips.

That kind 75-year-old man changed my day and enabled me to complete a half-Ironman. Help is often in the most unlikely places. Interestingly, once you commit to walk wounded, the universe often delivers help. We, however, must be both humble and brave enough to accept it.

Remember, when you can't do something, it doesn't mean you are flawed or broken. It simply means you have not yet stumbled on the best way to approach it. Keep trying different ways. Commit to the process. Ask for help.

I never thought I'd say this, but I love swimming now. I now have a sport I can do till I'm 100. It is far easier on my body than running 100-mile races. See what I mean? Often the hardest paths lead to the easiest trails. Dig in and commit to doing that thing you're afraid of.

CHAPTER 18

Abundant Thinking

WHEN I WAS GROWING UP, MY MOTHER HAD A HUGE LIBRARY OF books. She had a variety of self-help books. "Think and Grow Rich" was one. I remember thinking, "How exactly does that work? And why isn't she rich? Should she read it again?" I later read the book but it took quite a while before I was able to put it into action. I grew up poor. Really poor. As in sometimes we didn't have hot water or a phone line poor. I gratefully launched myself into my first job at 14, thrilled to be able to buy necessities for myself. From 14 to 35 I almost never missed a day at my many different jobs. I worked my way through junior college, and then nursing school and law school. I was constantly reinventing myself, adding new skills, education and licenses and trying to figure out how to go from poverty to upper class. By 35 I had achieved a reasonably comfortable middle class. I had paid off some of my law school debt by flipping houses on the side, while working as a full-time lawyer. My salary wasn't great, as, surprisingly, is the case with most lawyers. A handful of lawyers fare very well. Most do not. I was living in a small town with a big law school. Competition was intense and pay was low.

I remember being tired. I went for a run one day and as I was running, I mentally calculated my debts. The number I came up with seemed staggering. Outside of my home, I owed around $80,000 on student loans, vehicles, and credit cards. I tried to do the math on how long it would take me to pay all that off if I kept paying what my current budget allowed. It was a demoralizing thought. Too long. Many years. I didn't even know where or how to start.

I started listening to Dave Ramsey on the radio. He was talking about the "latte factor" and how saving $3 or $4 here could really add up and be a financial gamechanger. That math didn't seem to make sense either. What I didn't yet realize was that Dave Ramsey hit the nail on the head. The universe works in interesting ways. It works based on effort and commitment. When you fully trust and make the commitment, and put forth the effort and sacrifice, somehow the stars always align. I have seen it over and repeatedly.

I began doing the things he said. I decided to fully commit and trust the process. I started taking my lunch to work to save money. I picked one credit card and put all my energy into paying just that one bill off. As I started to do that, other ideas began popping into my head of how I could save here or earn more there. Then the financial opportunities, opportunities I had never ever had before, started trickling in. A partner at my law office asked me to help him with a case, and a few months later gave me a big cut. Totally unexpected. This had never happened to me before!

From there came the Masterminds group, two amazing job opportunities flowing in out of nowhere and less than a year later I found myself in my dream job, making three times the salary I had before. A few short years after that, not only was all my debt paid off, but my home was too. Change can happen fast, very fast, when you open your heart to it and fully commit. I never in a million years could have dreamed that I would be debt free by 40. But it happened. Oddly enough, by the time I received the dream job opportunity, I had already paid off most of my debt simply by changing my habits and following the principles of Dave Ramsey. The high paying job didn't save my financial struggles, strategic discipline did. The job was the cherry on the top.

Abundant thinking is magical. Keeping your brain clear of too many thoughts is also magical. One of the biggest zappers of energy and motivation is having too many thoughts swirling around in our minds. I refer to this as monkey brain. If you have thousands of thoughts racing around, it's hard to funnel any of them into real action. It makes you feel tired without having accomplished much. This is why meditation and intention are so heavily practiced by extremely successful people.

Here's a tip, any time you have a thought, try to handle and dispose of that thought immediately. If it is something you can act on and resolve immediately, do so. If not, write it down. Keep your brain as empty as possible. This helps you be present, appreciate the moment and circumstance in front of you, and be open to new information flowing in. This creates abundant thinking and helps you work smarter and more efficiently.

Last, try to find a purpose from every obstacle. Even if you must manufacture one, do it. Your brain believes your thoughts. Opportunities then flow to you from the thoughts you think, the energy you send out. The next time a frustrating event happens to you, smile. Shake your head and laugh and figure out one good thing that could happen because of this annoying situation. Recently my daughter was incredibly frustrated because one of her social media accounts was hacked. She was unable to access four years of photos, videos, and data that she did not have stored anywhere else. She was literally beside herself. I listened to her vent, I validated her feelings, and I expressed empathy. I told her I would help her figure out how to get it unlocked. Then, after setting that context, I told her, "You know, it's possible the universe wanted you to be social media free for a bit. There could be a reason. See if you can find the reason. Be curious. Be grateful for adversity, just as much as you are grateful for abundance. That is character." She looked at me dubiously. Over the next several days, I put a great deal of effort into helping her try to figure out how to fix it. Why? Because it wasn't just a social media account. It was something that meant a lot to her. I want my daughters to always know that what is important to them is important to me. Because they are important to me.

She researched and worked on that account for days and eventually fixed it. More importantly, it was something we bonded over. We were sad, determined and then jubilant together. These opportunities are the ones you'll remember forever. Never lose an opportunity to make the most of adversity.

CHAPTER 19

Lessons from Kevin and Kyle

RECENTLY I FOSTERED TWO PUPPIES FROM THE HUMANE SOCIETY. They are adorable. And loud. And needy. And I have realized something. Their urge for constant affection and attention is so strong that it must be managed. There are times when I have fed them, taken them out, played with them and finally put them back in the playpen for a nap only to be thanked by a cacophony of wails and crying fits. It's fascinating. Is this how the universe feels? I look at them and think, *"You're fine. Can you not just "be"? Just be grateful to have your brother and to be in a warm cozy bed with a blanket and toys and lots of love? Can you stop for five seconds and just relish that? Without screaming in fear that I might leave you and never return?*

This concept of acceptance is one the monks have perfected that most of us humans have not. When the pups stop the incessant howling and sit sweetly, grateful to just be in the moment, I am drawn to them and want to lavish them with play and love. Perhaps the universe feels the same? Perhaps it (or our family, friends, employer) cringes when we are unnecessarily whiny and smiles when we show gratitude and joy, despite uncertain circumstances?

As I leave to go to work and they cry, I wonder what they are thinking. Are they like humans? Are their little minds looping on why I'm so mean and how could I abandon them and are they not worthy or valued? When the fact is, it's not even about them! I just need to go to work! They simply need to learn how to self-soothe. No one is responsible for their feelings as I leave for work except them.

It's their responsibility to go find their cozy bed and take a nap, or go find one of their many chew toys and have some fun or frankly just choose to be calm and happy until I get home. How many times do some people get stuck in this same trap? Agonizing over someone else's lack of attention or affection when it's not even about them? Feeling unworthy or unloved when it's not even warranted? How much energy do we, like the puppies, waste on this when we could just be in the moment and chill?

Here's how this works:

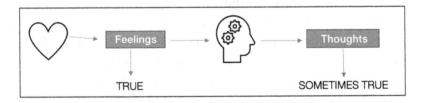

Feelings come from the heart. They are always true. They simply are what they are.

Thoughts come from the brain. They are the meaning we assign to a feeling, based on our prior conditioning, genetics, environment, and level of emotional maturity.

The question to ask yourself is this. Does my thought serve me? Not whether it is true or false, but does it serve me? If the thought does not serve you, can you reframe it in a way that does serve you?

Let's take an example. Perhaps when you look at your spouse, you feel contempt in your heart. And perhaps you feel that way because a thought you have had is that they are overweight and lazy. This is an ego driven, lower emotional maturity thought. It is judgmental, perhaps even self-righteous. Having this feeling in your heart and this thought in your mind will certainly affect the way you react to and communicate with your spouse. Does this thought serve you? Or them? Or the relationship? Even if it is true, is it not destructive? What purpose does it serve other than to further self-inflate your own sense of superiority?

An empathy driven, higher emotional maturity thought is to acknowledge the contempt laden feeling and go deeper to ask yourself why it is there. What is being triggered within you? Usually when we are triggered by others, it is because of some deeper baggage we do not like about ourselves. Perhaps we resent that we are so hard on ourselves, and we want to be more like our carefree spouse who enjoys ice cream. Once we resolve where our feelings truly originate, the empathy driven thought can then be reframed to be useful. "I wonder why my spouse seems less motivated than they used to be. I wonder if I could be supportive in a different or better way. I could ask them if they are happy and if they feel supported by me. I could focus on their good points and stop focusing on their flaws. After all, we have flaws. Perhaps theirs is weight and perhaps mine is being judgmental and being too hard on myself and others. Perhaps I could work to be kinder to myself and others. Perhaps I need to be less concerned about my spouse's flaws and more focused on their strengths." This is an example of a mature thought process that serves you and works to the benefit of all.

Here's another example. You're driving down the road and someone almost swerves into you. You feel adrenaline and fear in your heart.

A person of ego driven low emotional maturity thinks: "That MF is trying to kill me!! I'll show him! I'm going to flip him off and chase him down and make him suffer!" This is a toxic response that causes everyone to suffer, especially the person who is thinking about it.

A person of empathy driven high emotional maturity thinks: "Yikes, that was close. They must have been distracted for a minute." This person goes on about their day with no vengefulness and no emotional energy wasted on this unimportant situation. As a result, they have more energy to pour into creative, productive endeavors.

Years ago, I frequently had the thought, "I'm not creative." I had no idea where that thought came from. Where do ridiculous self-limiting thoughts like this arise? One day, I had that thought, and my next thought was, "Says who?" "Who decided I'm not creative? Me? Based on what? Because I couldn't make a sculpture from a bar of soap in that summer camp? Seriously? Have I been basing it on that embarrassing memory??" My next thought was this: There are many forms of creativity. I am really good at solving difficult problems at work that other people can't resolve. That is another form of creativity. I AM creative. I begin thinking about this regularly. I AM creative. This new image of myself became fun. I would be confronted with a scenario requiring imagination or creativity and I would get excited. "Let's see what I can do," I would think excitedly. Rather than comparing myself to others, I began to feel a genuine curiosity to explore my own yet untapped abilities. Today, I think of myself as a highly creative problem solver. It has released blocks and generally made my life a lot more fun.

Make a list of all the self-limiting thoughts you have about yourself.

_____

_____

_____

Ask yourself whether you want to keep them. Are they serving you? Or is it time to trade them in for some more useful thoughts, ones that could set you free and make your life a lot more exciting and fun? Pick one and follow the steps to reframe it, act on it, and develop a new belief. Write it out here.

_____

_____

Last example. Another thing I've never been able to do is pull-ups. For some reason, there is a pervasive thought in my head that I can't, therefore I literally almost will not even try. I bought a pull up bar. Tried it a few times and gave up. Because I can't do pull-ups...right? Joined CrossFit to see if they could teach me. Found myself skipping every class where pullups were listed on the workout of the day. Because the thought was controlling my actions. One day I realized this was simply another example of a limiting thought. For the first time ever, I changed my thought. "I can do pull-ups. I just do not know how yet." Because the new thought was more liberating, it occurred to me to google how to do pull-ups. It said to start by using a step stool so that it would be easier to jump up and hold with chin above the bar. It said to jump up, hold, and come down as slowly as possible. A negative pull-up. Oh. Well, that I can do. And so, I did. I started doing just one negative pull up every time I was in the vicinity of my pull-up bar. That's it. Just one negative. Days turned into weeks. Weeks turned into months. This is how change happens. We start with the small thing we can do and build on that.

Every time we confront one of our self-limiting thoughts head-on and reframe them, we find ourselves suddenly motivated to take action. Once we take action, we build self-confidence. The former Navy Seal David Goggins is a phenomenal example of this. He was overweight and ridden with self-limiting thoughts. He confronted them, plotted out a methodical plan, tricked his brain into motivation and now he is unbelievably self-disciplined and, as a result, self-confident. He is limitless. You can be, too.

EXERCISE:

Close your eyes and empty your thoughts. Look at the blackness. Let your eyes stroll down the tunnel of darkness. Breathe as your eyes stroll, looking around the blackness. Picture ocean waves surging in and cleansing your brain of ALL thoughts, leaving it fresh and clean and new.

Every time I do this, I feel my body relax, a weight being lifted off, and am flooded with creative new ideas and possibilities.

All this to say, most puppies figure this out quickly. They learn to feel the feeling of anxiety as you walk out the door and replace their thought from "she's never coming back" to a thought of "she'll be back later, I'm safe." They find ways to entertain themselves until you are back. This is maturity. Dogs are also almost always joyful and unconditional in their love, each time you return. Be more like the mature versions of Kyle and Kevin.

CHAPTER 20

Who Do You Want to Be

YOU DO NOT GET WHAT YOU DESERVE IN THIS LIFE, YOU GET WHAT you fight for. This physical life comes with all sorts of never-ending hurdles, challenges, and setbacks. It's not easy. These struggles, though, are what mold us and change us if we allow them. We can chalk these life events up to adversity and feel victimized, or we can accept the hardship, look for the lesson, grow through it and be determined to thrive regardless.

The happiest, most driven people haven't had adversity free lives. They just did not let those adversities be their focus. They navigated them and chose to keep a strong mindset. This helped unleash their creativity, which helped them find ways to make lemonade out of lemons.

We all tend to think a lot about what we should do. We do not think as much as about who we want to be. What character traits do we want to be known for? Loving? Funny? Resilient? Vibrant? Kind? Honest? Ethical? Try to come up with three-character traits that are important to you and that you want to be known for. Then think about things you can do and say to leave that legacy of who you are. That is, after all, while we are here. To evolve and grow and leave a legacy of who we became, in such a way that it impacts others.

Once you focus on who you want to be, it starts becoming much easier to determine what to do, and how to craft goals.

Someone once asked me what career path I followed to become a COO of a healthcare company. The fact is, it had never occurred to me to be a COO of anything. I was interested in medicine and wanted to go to medical school. I had no money or family financial support so I knew I would have to work my way through it. I went to nursing school so that I could work as a nurse through med school. Along the way, I decided on law school. I worked my way through law school as a nurse. After law school, I was in debt, so I began flipping houses on the side to help pay off loans. Then I opened a retail store for the same reason. That failed, but it taught me a lot about running a business. I practiced law for many years, changing my practice area as the market demands changed. I practiced a good bit of healthcare related law and one day received an opportunity to manage the legal dept of a healthcare company. I took that position but then continually offered to help with any other needs of the company. Over time, they gave me additional departments. Clinical, payroll, human resources. I was very willing to work extra and to work outside the scope of my job description. As a result, before long I was running all the operations. It became my dream job. The point is this. Just lay a brick every day. Be willing to give more than you're being paid for. Be curious about other roles. Take risks to take on projects you may not fully know how to do. Before long, it becomes something. It all starts with who you're willing to be and what you're willing to do.

What can you learn about today? What new skill can you work on? How do you want to show up each day, in your career and your relationships? Who do you want to be?

What is the one Thing you want to overcome or change this month?

I hope that life can become like an epic video game for you. One where you are curious about what lies behind each door, where you are brave enough to fight demons, where you are willing to pick a new story and where you make choices to move from ego to empathy.

Work smarter. Live freely. Create legacy.

END

Printed in the United States
by Baker & Taylor Publisher Services